INSIGHT COMPACT GUIDES

Gran

Compact Guide: Gran Canaria is the ideal quick-reference guide to this favourite holiday destination. It tells you all you need to know about the island's attractions, from sun-drenched beaches to rugged valleys and canyons, from the bustle of the resorts to the peace of ancient caves and forests.

This is just one title in *Apa Publications'* new series of pocket-sized, easy-to-use guidebooks intended for the independent-minded traveller. *Compact Guides* pride themselves on being up-to-date and authoritative. They are in essence mini travel encyclopedias, designed to be comprehensive yet portable, as well as readable and reliable.

Star Attractions

An instant reference to some of Gran Canaria's most popular tourist attractions to help you on your way.

Casa Colón, Las Palmas p24

Calle Mayor de Triana, Las Palmas p26

Playa de las Canteras p30

Agaete p40

Dedo de Dios p42

Barranco de Guayadeque p48

Maspalomas dunes p53

Playa de San Nicolás p61

Puerto de Mogán p56

San Bartolomé de Tirjana p65

Pinar de Tamadaba p68

Gran Canaria

Gran Canaria – A Continent in Miniature

Playa de la Aldea

Tempting slogans such as 'The Longest Beaches in Europe' with promises of 'Eternal Spring' adorn the tour operators' brochures. More disparaging headlines and gossip might refer to the concrete jungle in Maspalomas or to tourists wasting the island's precious water resources. Empty promises by the tour operators, or exaggerated prophecies of doom? Both attitudes contain elements of truth: there is more than one side to this miniature paradise off the coast of Africa.

Gran Canaria, the focal point of the Canary Islands archipelago, is an island of great beauty, although this fact may not be immediately apparent, particularly when you're on the bus from the airport to Las Palmas. The landscape ranges from the endless sandy beaches of the south coast to the dramatic gorges and rock formations of the mountainous interior. Beyond the resorts, there are sleepy fishing villages waiting to be discovered, Andalusian-style historic town centres to admire, abandoned cave dwellings to marvel at and little squares for simply dozing under shady bay trees. Gran Canaria is both overcrowded and deserted: the visitor can get lost on a lonely beach or plunge into the nightlife of an international resort. While people bask in the sun at Playa del Inglés, snow can cap the peaks around Tejeda barely 40km (25 miles) inland.

Luxuriant Las Palmas

Paternal support

The Canary Islanders themselves are likeable. Their openness towards visitors perhaps stems from the fact that for centuries, their islands, important as a strategic port of call, have been in constant communication with other parts of the world. The strong trading links that were established between the Canary Islands, Europe, America and Africa were to bring people of all nations to these shores. They have come and gone and come and stayed, and visitors today will receive no less a welcome.

Location and size

Gran Canaria is part of the Spanish autonomous region of the Canary Islands and is the third largest island in the archipelago (after Tenerife and Fuerteventura). The archipelago comprises the islands of Lanzarote, Fuerteventura and Gran Canaria to the east, and Tenerife, La Gomera, La Palma and El Hierro to the west. Gran Canaria lies some 63km (39 miles) from Tenerife and 197km (123 miles) from the African mainland on a level with southern Morocco. The island is almost a perfect circle in shape and covers an area of 1,560sq km (602sq miles); its diameter at its widest point is 53.4km (33½ miles). The highest mountain is the Pico de las Nieves (1,949m/ 6,395ft).

5

Dedo de Dios

Geology and landscape

As recently as the 1960s, experts were still divided as to what caused this island to be formed some 16 million years ago. Today it has been established that Gran Canaria is neither a broken-off segment of the African mainland, nor is it the remains of some sunken continent. The island, like all the Canary Islands, was formed by volcanic activity beneath the Atlantic Ocean. Continental drift made the ocean bed of the Atlantic particularly unstable in the region of the Canary Islands. The formation of the island is reflected in the landscape. The oldest part of the island is the mountain massif in the centre which was formed by earth movements during a succession of volcanic eruptions. The lava flows carved deep trenches in the rock strata, which can still be seen in the form of gorges (*barrancos*), and deposited fertile soil in the northern part of the island. The vast stretches of sand on the south coast, on the other hand, resulted from changes in sea level following the Ice Age. The white sandy beaches were not, as is often claimed, blown across from the Sahara but were washed ashore by the sea. The sand dunes of Maspalomas are formed of nothing but the remains of crustaceans, ground to a fine powder over the millennia.

Enjoying the eternal spring

Climate and when to go

Gran Canaria's much-praised 'eternal spring' is actually a warm early summer. Temperatures rarely rise above 26°C (79°F); only in August does the thermometer soar somewhat higher. Furthermore, there is usually a gentle breeze, and the nightly minimum temperature rarely sinks below 15°C (59°F). Correspondingly, the water temperature seldom falls below 19°C (66°F), even in winter.

These perennial summer-like temperatures are a result of the northeast trade wind, a constant current of air which is warmed up over the Caribbean and blows along the same route across the northern hemisphere every day of the year. Reaching the Canary Islands from a north-easterly direction and thus bringing cooler air, the wind is also responsible for bringing the clouds which pass uneventfully across the low-lying islands of Lanzarote and Fuerteventura, but deposit their rain when they reach the higher central massif of Gran Canaria (1,900m/ 6,000ft). The northern half of the island is frequently not only cloudy but also cooler than the rest. Above the favoured holiday resorts in the southern half of the island the sun is rarely obscured by the trade-wind clouds. Temperatures here are thus appreciably higher.

This stable pattern dominates the weather of Gran Canaria for about 300 days of the year. Between November and January there may be short, heavy showers of rain when an Atlantic trough forces the trade winds back, while a Sahara sandstorm may force its way across in the face of the trade winds during the summer months. When this happens temperatures may soar for two or three days to around 40°C (104°F) whilst the warm *levante* wind whips sand from the Sahara across the island. The locals refer to this phenomenon as 'Africa weather' (*tiempo africano*).

The Canary Islands, especially Gran Canaria, are almost always in season. Central Europeans come in spring, autumn and winter, when it is cold at home, whilst the Spanish come in summer when the Iberian peninsula is too hot. Older people favour the climate because the low diurnal temperature range (annual average 7°C/13°F) places no strain on the heart and circulatory system. The *levante*, however, can be troublesome for those suffering from respiratory problems. If you wish to avoid this problem you should not travel to Gran Canaria during July and August. No one, however, should be dissuaded by the prospect of rain from visiting the archipelago in winter.

A shady spot in Telde

Even during November and January, the wettest months, there is rarely more than 30mm (1.2 in) of rain on the coast. The most popular time to visit Gran Canaria is usually the week before Easter and the Easter period itself, as well as the Spanish holiday months of July and August and the period between Christmas and the New Year. Those wishing to enjoy the Canary Islands in relative peace and quiet and with the weather at its best are recommended to visit the archipelago during May, June and October. These are also the months during which the hotels offer the most favourable terms.

7

Flora

As can be expected of a 'miniature continent', the vegetation of Gran Canaria is extremely varied, ranging from the Canary pine trees in the higher central areas to the palms and exotic fruit trees such as mangos, pawpaws and avocados in the south. It should be noted, however, that none of the magnificent decorative plants, including hibiscus, bougainvillaea, oleander, begonia, the bird of paradise flower and a variety of acacias and poinsettias, which are lovingly nurtured in Gran Canaria's parks and gardens, are native to the island. They have all been imported at some time or another from distant tropical or subtropical countries. Thanks to the climate, however, they are invariably healthier and bigger than the equivalent northern European specimens.

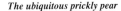

The ubiquitous prickly pear

Those endemic species still to be found on the island are not, in the main, tremendously exciting or beautiful to look at. In the hot, dry zone, below 400m (1,300ft), the local plants have developed a variety of methods of surviving. In order to minimise the loss of moisture through transpiration, many plants have narrow leaves, or

Some plants are more flamboyant than others

have developed a hard wooden exterior. Others transform their moisture into a thick sap. Succulents of the euphorbia family contain a white milky sap which is a strong irritant. Typical species to be found in the arid zone are *Cardón cardonales*, or pillar euphorbia (commonly known as the candelabra cactus), which looks like it must be a native of Mexico but in fact abounds in the south of Gran Canaria, reaching tremendous heights. The *tabaiba* is a common shrub with narrow leaves, resembling a miniature tree. The other cactus-like plant commonly found on the hillsides and bordering the road towards the north and centre of the island is the prickly pear (*Opuntia ficus indica*), which was brought to the Canaries from Mexico in the 16th century. For many years it became an essential part of the island's economy. The plants were used to cultivate the cochineal, an insect whose larvae produce a red dye and was bought in huge quantities at the Canary wharf during the late 18th and early 19th centuries, before man-made dyes came on the scene. There has recently been an upturn in demand for the cochineal, and new prickly pear plantations have been created in response, particularly on Lanzarote.

The distinctive dragon-tree (*Dracena draco*) is closely related to the yucca. It is commonly found in the central upper regions of the island. The dragon-tree, with its dark green sword-shaped leaves, formed an essential part of the original inhabitants' religious beliefs and was a vital ingredient in their medicinal remedies.

The Canary date-palm (*Phoenix canariensis*) is a close relative of the date palm of North Africa and the Arab countries, but has larger, more luxuriant leaves. Mostly found in the south of the island, it bears a small date-like fruit known as the *tamara*, which is, however, inedible. It is interesting to watch the pruners at work as they scale

Canary pines

the rough trunk with the aid of a leather sling to 'shave the beards' of the emblematic trees, which appear on the coat-of-arms of Las Palmas de Gran Canaria.

Found in the mountainous interior, the Canary pine (*Pinus canariensis*) might be less majestic than its Nordic counterparts, but it thrives particularly well on these arid volcanic islands. Because its resinous sap is totally fire-proof, it invariably survives a forest fire. It is not unusual to see whole areas where the trunks of the trees stand in a charred wilderness, while up on high the green needles glisten in the sunlight. The needles, which are almost 30cm (12in) long and grow in clusters of three, are adapted to extract the maximum amount of water from the air, made moist by the clouds borne by the trade winds.

Native species forming the undergrowth in the island's pine forests include the *Amagantes*, a pink-flowering rock-rose, and *Codeso*, a leguminous plant which bears bright yellow blossoms in spring. Native to the mountainous interior is the imposing Canary *Toginaste*, which grows as high as two metres (6ft).

Of the lush forests which covered the island before the Spanish conquest, only a few square miles or about one percent of the original woodland remains in the north. This is the home of the Canary laurel tree (*laurus canariensis*), which grows in the cloud layer created by the trade winds and whose leaves are used for culinary purposes. One of the finest laurel forests is Los Tilos de Moya (*see page 11*).

Fauna

Although the flora of the Tertiary eras has survived on the Canary islands, visitors will be pleased to know that much of the fauna has not. One of the most delightful things about the archipelago in general is that there are no dangerous animals to be encountered anywhere, either on land or in the sea. The most common creature on Gran Canaria is the lizard (*lagarto*), which can often be spotted dashing from bush to bush. This endearing plant-eater should not be confused with the smaller *geckos* (*peringué*), which live on mosquitoes and which may even find their way into hotel bedrooms.

Visitors may be expecting to see 'ships of the desert' sitting round the dunes or chewing placidly in the fields. This is not the case. Although still employed in agriculture on Lanzarote, the few camels to be seen on Gran Canaria have been imported solely to entertain the tourists. The local canary bird (*canario*) is also something of a disappointment: although the Canary-Islands ancestor of our feathered friend sings as exquisitely as its domesticated counterpart, its greyish-green plumage is much less conspicuous. Smaller than a wren, the *capirote* has been nick-named the Canary nightingale; together with a number

9

A friendly native

of birds of prey (sparrowhawk, kestrel, buzzard and African vulture), it flourishes on Gran Canaria.

Visitors staying in the south of the island may well be treated to the nocturnal perambulations of the cockroaches, especially if there are gardens and bougainvillaea nearby. Walking barefoot in the dark is not advised.

The sea is also clear of danger, though sometimes visitors on the beach at Las Canteras may encounter nasty-looking jellyfish (known locally as *aguavivas*). In the rocky areas of the south coast you have to watch out for the *erizo del mar*, the 'sea hedgehog' which, as its name suggests, is dangerously prickly. But there are no sharks to worry about, and whales and dolphins are rarely sighted.

Environmental issues

Much of the coast is unspoilt

Las Palmas de Gran Canaria

Tourism, particularly of the sun-sea-and-sand variety, is always hard on an environment, and Gran Canaria's is no exception. However, the economic need to diversify in tourism while responding to environmental criticism is likely to produce a 'greener' future for the island. In recent years much has been done to ensure that the pristine quality of the seawater is maintained, mainly by exploring the possibilities of recycling waste waters and solids, while industries are endorsing energy-conscious programmes to improve their environmental image.

To anyone from colder climes, it must always have seemed a mystery that solar energy was not widely used on Gran Canaria. Now, particularly in the south of the island, much has been done to rectify this situation. Wind power has also experienced a sudden upturn in popularity as an alternative way producing electricity. Developments such as the windmill field at Pozo Izquierdo (where the annual windsurfing world championships are held) may not be as decorative or scenically beautiful as Don Quixote's famous windmill on La Mancha, but they are certainly highly efficient.

The autonomous government's new bills on energy production and use and protection of the coastline in the Canary Archipelago have gone a long way to ensuring that environmental issues feature high on everyone's agenda. Meanwhile, moves are still being made to convert more areas of the different islands into national parks, thereby precluding the possibility of land speculation and destruction. The National Park of Tejeda and Roque Nublo, although a subject of controversy, would appear to be a near reality, and the environmental groups are constantly exerting pressure to halt development in areas of great natural beauty such as Veneguera and Güigüi.

Environmental protection groups – Gran Canaria's AS-CAN is the largest in Spain – are becoming more active and influential. Companies associated with tourism have taken over the responsibility for financing parks and re-forestation projects. They also force town councils to adopt a more environmentally conscious approach in their planning schemes.

Some of the remaining natural wonders of Gran Canaria are inaccessible to tourists and Canary Islanders alike. The laurel forest of Los Tilos de Moya (*see page 9*), has been closed to the public in order to prevent further damage from weekend barbecues, etc. The woodland area around Inagua is totally off the beaten track and uninhabited and thus seems safe. Only the hikers who follow the newly traced *Caminos Reales* can penetrate this natural haven.

The Canary Islands in general suffer from a shortage of fresh water, in particular as a result of increased consumption during the past few years. Early explorers and other visitors confirm that the island was once green and water was plentiful. Rainfall, at an average of 576mm (23 inches), exceeds some places in England. Dense forests once covered Gran Canaria. Since the arrival of the Spanish, the destruction of the forests to make way for water-intensive farming crops – sugar cane, bananas and tomatoes – has greatly reduced the capacity of the soil to store water. The lowering of the water table exacerbates the problem as sea water seeps into the porous volcanic rock, making wells and watercourses brackish. Furthermore, traditional farming methods involve setting fire to areas of forest so that the new green shoots will provide fodder for goats.

Although the growing numbers of tourists place increasing demands on water supplies, farming still accounts for more than half the island's total water requirements. However, Gran Canaria is perhaps better equipped than anywhere else in Spain to meet present demands. Extensive research projects and the development of alternative ways of producing drinking and irrigation water have placed the island at the forefront of desalination and recycling technology. Many tomato plants are now irrigated with salt water, so you can forget the salt on your salads from now on.

Population and religion

More than 600,000 of the 1.7 million inhabitants of the Canary Islands live on the island of Gran Canaria – and more than 500,000 of these are clumped together in the capital, Las Palmas de Gran Canaria. Although Gran Canaria is only the third-largest island in the archipelago, it accounts for almost half of the total population and is thus the most densely inhabited island in the group. The busy port and tourism have attracted many of the 25,000 residents from other parts of the world who came to set up permanent residence on the island.

A precious commodity

11

Relaxing after a long day

A fishermen's shrine

The people of Gran Canaria, perhaps more than other Canary Islanders, have a highly cosmopolitan outlook. And, as behoves people who live in isolated regions, they are also community minded. Like any other Spaniards, they consider themselves first and foremost to be from their *patricia chica*, ie *canarión*.

The original cave-dwelling inhabitants were sun-worshippers and had their own pagan deities and rituals. Spanish supremacy made Roman Catholicism the only official religion, a situation that endured until the end of Franco's dictatorship. As in other parts of Spain, there are now large communities of Masons, Baptists, Mormons, Muslims, and Jehova's Witnesses besides the substantial body of Catholics.

Language

The official language on Gran Canaria is Spanish (*Castellano*). However, a strong local dialect is widely spoken; its main characteristics are the swallowing of final consonants, the increased use of the subjunctive and the adoption of South American vocabulary. Thus '*autobus*' becomes '*guagua*', and '*patata*' (potato) becomes '*papa*'. English and German are widely understood and spoken in tourist centres.

Economy

Because of its distance from the mainland, the Canary archipelago always enjoyed special status within the Spanish state. When the import and export trade was set up by British entrepreneurs, the islands were awarded the status of duty-free ports, a situation which persisted from the 19th century until full integration with the European Union in 1996. Now, the geographical isolation of the archipelago means it qualifies to be treated as a peripheral area within the EU, which entitles it to various subsidies and aid programmes.

For a long time, the Puerto de la Luz at Las Palmas was the island's only link with the outside world, and much of Gran Canaria's economic activity is still closely linked to the port. As part of a vast modernisation project, the harbour moles have recently been extended. The reorganisation has also led to a major facelift being carried out on the Parque Santa Catalina, in the port area, where the British merchants, Elder and Miller, erected the first export/import warehouses and offices. This is the first area to be explored by many cruise parties which stop off at Las Palmas de Gran Canaria.

Tourism: Together with the port activity, Gran Canaria's main source of direct and indirect employment comes from tourism, which accounts for more than 70 percent of GDP. The main nerve centre of tourism is on the

The port is vital

The masses of Maspalomas

southern stretch of coast between San Agustín and Puerto de Mogán. The tourism on offer is sea, sun, sand and sometimes sex. However, a lot of EU money has been ploughed into rural options to the north – luxury cave dwellings to rent for a romantic weekend and rural hotels offering activity programmes from language courses to hiking and transcendental meditation. There is also a rising interest in conference tourism.

Although most tourism is located in the south, most of the inhabitants of Gran Canaria – at least 500,000 people – live in the capital, Las Palmas de Gran Canaria, in the north of the island. Just as well, then, that EU funds have been put to good use in enlarging the infrastructure – roads, airports, hospital facilities, desalination plants and the like – necessary to support a massive influx of visitors (over 3.5 million per year).

With a firm and long-standing tradition of quality tourism for more than thirty years, Gran Canaria is now shaping up in preparation for new trends in international tourism. Greater emphasis is being laid on the desirability of resurrecting the island's cultural heritage, such as the various festivals and celebrations, and in rediscovering the pre-Hispanic history of the island archipelago in an attempt to show visitors how distinct the roots of the Canary Islanders are from their present-day countrymen, the Spaniards.

Agriculture and industry: Sugar cane, the first agricultural export of an island with no natural resources, was introduced by the Spanish and exported after processing. However, competition from the cheaper sugar of Central America meant production began to decline in the 16th century. Wine was subsequently cultivated and the Canary Malvasía (Malmsey) wine was sold all over Europe. The 19th century saw the rearing of the cochineal as a major branch of the economy, but its importance declined with the advent of aniline dyes (*see page 8*). Bananas were introduced from Indochina and subsequently marketed by the British in the 19th century. But in recent years, banana growing, too, has been in a state of crisis. The quality of the Canary Island banana is more than a match for its Central American counterpart, but its small size means that it is almost unsaleable in the European market. In addition, production costs are much higher than in other countries. It takes 400 litres (88 gallons) of expensive irrigation water for the Campesino on Gran Canaria to harvest of 1kg of bananas. In the tropical climate of Costa Rica, on the other hand, no irrigation is necessary at all, and wages are also considerably lower.

Bananas face an uncertain future

Spain guaranteed a market for the bananas, but only up to the end of 1995, a transition period of ten years after it joined the EU. After this period, Spain was obliged to admit bananas from other countries. As a result, banana plantations have increasingly given way to exotic vegetables, cut flowers and pot plants.

Gran Canaria is the Canary Islands' largest producer of tomatoes for the European market. However, the tomato is suffering a similar fate to that already suffered by the banana. Thanks to their low labour costs, countries such as Morocco have made dramatic inroads into the Canary Islands' markets – including the EU. It is not unusual to see piles of tomatoes being dumped by their disgruntled farmers as a protest against European rulings, quotas and lack of protectionism.

Until the beginning of the 1990s, the largest foreign contingent on the island was Korean, mainly due to the marked dominance of the Korean fishing fleet in Puerto de la Luz. But port conditions and EU restrictions on fishing have resulted in the exodus of this fleet and created severe hardship in this sector of the economy as a whole.

Puerto de Mogán

Despite the problems outlined above, not all is doom and gloom. The transition from belonging to Spain to forming part of the EU has been relatively untraumatic for the Canary Islands. The smoothness with which the islanders have adapted to the new circumstances is hardly surprising. They are used to adopting policies imposed from the outside by the central government in Spain, and a large part of the population either is foreign or is used to working with and for foreigners.

Industry is gradually picking up on Gran Canaria. Obviously, the distance from markets and high transport costs have been weighty factors in dissuading industry from establishing itself on the island. However, the collaboration of the university (formed by popular demand in 1990) with industry, above all in the fields of energy production, bodes favourably for the future. Fish farming and the commercial development of seaweed derivatives are two of the successful joint ventures undertaken to date.

Diversifying into new crops

Politics and Administration

Each island forms an administrative unit, whilst the archipelago is divided into two provinces which together combine to form an autonomous region.

15

The *Cabildo Insular* is the administrative body on each island and is responsible for all decisions above town or village level. It deals, for example, with questions of road construction or environmental protection.

Las Palmas is also the capital of the province of the same name, to which the islands of Lanzarote and Fuerteventura also belong. The second province based on Tenerife covers the remaining four islands. In addition, Las Palmas is the capital and seat of government of the 'Autonomous Region of the Canary Islands', which was formed in 1982 and which includes both provinces. The rivalry between the individual islands can be seen in the fact that, although the government has its seat in Las Palmas, the regional parliament is situated in Santa Cruz de Tenerife.

The Canary Islands tend to spring political surprises on a fairly regular basis. After the return of democracy, calls for an independent Canary archipelago were first voiced by a small left-wing separatist minority. Soon afterwards the moderate right-wing party ATI was formed *(Asociación Tinerfeña Independiente)*, with demands that the Canaries' special status should be recognised; it was particularly successful in local elections.

The latest political development is the *Coalición Canaria*, formed in 1993, a colourful coalition of communists, left- and right-wing nationalists and separatists, all of them separate from the PSOE (Spain's ruling social democratic party) and all of them united in order to protect 'Canarian interests'.

Historical Highlights

c 3000BC Settlement starts on Canary Islands. Finds suggest that the earliest inhabitants are Cro-Magnon people who could have come from the African mainland. They are later followed by at least one more wave of settlers, probably from the Mediterranean area.

From 1200BC Regular visits by the Phoenicians and later the Carthaginians, but no trading contacts are established with the original inhabitants, who continue to follow their Stone-Age lifestyle until the Spanish conquest.

25BC According to an account written by Pliny the Elder, King Juba II of Numidia and Mauritania, appointed by Rome, has the Canaries explored. Remains of buildings, but no people, are discovered on the eastern islands of Lanzarote and Fuerteventura.

AD150 The Greek geographer Ptolemy shows the islands on his map of the world. The map shows the westernmost edge of the world (his prime meridian) running through the western tip of the island of El Hierro.

1312 The eastern Canary Islands are accidentally rediscovered by a Genoese of Provençal origin named Lanzarote Malocello, when his ship is driven off course on a journey to England. He spends almost 20 years on the island that is later named after him.

1341 Boccaccio mentions four Canarian slaves, goatskins, tallow, red-dyed wood and red earth brought back by the Genoese steersman Niccoloso da Recco. This visit is followed by several plundering expeditions by Genoese, Catalan, Majorcan and Basque seafarers.

1344 Luís de la Cerda, scion of the Spanish House of Castile, is appointed king of the Canary Islands by Pope Clement VI. However, this is only a title and doesn't imply possession. He never sets foot on the islands.

1391 Thirteen monks sent to the Canary Islands to spread Christianity are murdered. This is followed by a bloody campaign of revenge against the local population, after which the survivors are imprisoned and enslaved.

1402–6 Robert of Bracamonte, presented with the still-independent Canary Islands by Henry III of Castile, hands them on to his French cousin, Jean de Béthencourt. The latter claims the islands of Lanzarote, Fuerteventura, El Hierro and later La Gomera on behalf of Spain, but fails in his attempt to take Gran Canaria.

1477–83 A Spanish force led by Juan Rejón lands on Gran Canaria. The island is ruled by two chiefs, Tenesor Semidan in the west and Doramas in the east. In 1478, the Spanish found the town of Las Palmas and embark on their conquest. Tenesor Samidan sides with the Spaniards, but many of the native inhabitants pursue a bitter struggle against the invaders. They are finally subdued by the forces of Pedro de Vera and Alonso Fernández de Lugo.

1480 Under the terms of the Treaty of Toledo, Portugal's claim to the Canary Islands is finally abandoned.

1492 After a brief stopover on the island of La Gomera, Christopher Columbus sails on to the west and discovers America.

1494–6 After suffering initial defeat at Matanza de Acentejo, Alonso Fernández de Lugo succeeds after three more campaigns in wresting Tenerife from the Guanches, who have been weakened by a plague epidemic. In the decades that follow, the Canary Islands gradually become an indispensable sea base for trips to America.

c 1500 Sugar cane forms the first monoculture and first agricultural product. Merchants from Seville make vast profits; the work is undertaken by black and white slaves. Las Palmas becomes a slave market. From 1554, the sugar-cane industry declines as a result of competition from the West Indies and Brazil.

From 1543 The capture of the fortress of La Isleta, originally built to protect Las Palmas, marks the beginning of a series of pirate raids over the next two hundred years. French, British, Dutch and Berber fleets sail between the islands. Las Palmas is the subject of the most severe attack when it is stormed by the forces of Johan van der Does, a Dutch buccaneer.

1700–1950 Poverty repeatedly forces many of the Canary Islanders to emigrate. Cuba and Venezuela are favoured destinations.

1830 A short economic boom follows the introduction of the cochineal, an insect whose larvae produce a valuable red dye. The prosperity is brought to an end by the invention of aniline dyes.

1852 Isabella II declares the Canary Islands a free-trade zone.

1890 The British introduce bananas as a monoculture on the archipelago.

1912 Limited self-administration councils – *cabildos insulares* – are allowed on the islands.

1927 The Canary Islands are divided into two provinces. Santa Cruz de Tenerife becomes the capital of the western province, and Las Palmas de Gran Canaria capital of the eastern province.

1936 On July 17 Francisco Bahamonde Franco, the military governor of the Canary Islands, initiates the Spanish Civil War from his residence in Tenerife. Three days later the islands are in the hands of the Fascists.

1956 The first charter plane lands on Gran Canaria. Since this time, tourism has developed into by far the most important industry. In 1974 the international airport at Gando is opened.

1978–82 Following the death of Franco and the restoration of the monarchy, the new Spanish constitution joins the two Canary Islands provinces to form the 'Autonomous Region of the Canary Islands'.

1986 Spain joins the European Union and negotiates a special status for the Canary Islands until the end of 1995.

1993 The 'Coalición Canaria', a union of regional parties of the right and left, topples the local parliamentary president. In the national elections on 6 June, the coalition wins four seats and thus becomes the sixth-strongest party in the national parliament in Madrid.

end of 1995 The Canary Islands are fully integrated into the European Union. The islands' free-trade status is in jeopardy.

The Guanches

Much has been discovered about the Stone Age culture of the original Canary Islanders, or Guanches. The name originated on Tenerife and means 'sons of the earth'; it is now used as the general term for the original inhabitants of all the islands. The Guanches mummified their dead and buried them in caves. The mummies so far discovered – and also the little written evidence that remains – have led scientists to place the original islanders' ethnic origins in Northwest Africa. Some runes scratched on a stone discovered a few years ago in Tenerife have been transliterated as *zanata*, which is also the name of a Berber tribe, but this is speculation. Later settlers had distinctly Mediterranean features.

Language, political organisation and culture varied from island to island. On Gran Canaria there was a hereditary monarchy and an aristocracy into which citizens could be elected. The leader of the noblemen was the *Fayan*, who combined the role of chief judge and high priest. The *Fayan* was often a woman.

The organisation of the state was remarkably democratic, and private life was based on equality. Marriage and divorce laws were liberal, and women fought alongside men in battle.

The Guanches did not know the wheel, nor did they use bows and arrows, and there is no firm evidence that they could sail. As there are no iron deposits on the island they continued to live in the Stone Age until medieval times. They mostly lived in groups of caves, in which an entire village could be housed. Only when space became limited did they build stone houses, whose design can be deduced from the natural stone dwellings that are still in use all over the Canary Islands.

The Guanches lived on wild fruits and berries. There was no game, so pigs, sheep, goats and dogs provided not only meat but also the materials for covers and clothes. Fish also formed a part of their diet, as did dates, mushrooms and roots. The national dish, *gofio*, was originally prepared from fern roots.

What became of the Guanches? Those who were not butchered or sold into slavery by the Spanish mixed with the colonisers. Nonetheless, many inhabitants of Gran Canaria claim to be directly descended from the Guanches. This seems unlikely, but it demonstrates the trend towards maintaining a distinct cultural identity. A book was recently published containing Guanche names, and babies are once more called Tamara or Tanausu.

Playa de las Canteras

20

The Guanche monument

Route 1

★★★ Las Palmas de Gran Canaria

Capital city, port, trading centre, metropolis, garden city, shopping mecca: Las Palmas has something of everything. There are six-lane urban motorways and narrow streets in which the traffic builds up into traffic jams. High-rise developments overlook the town from the surrounding mountains and make you think of Manhattan. Elegant department stores, ancient covered markets and street traders recall those of Rio or Cannes, while Las Canteras bay, one of the largest natural swimming pools in the world, stands comparison with Copacabana. The best way to discover the many faces of Las Palmas is on foot. You should allow a full day in order to explore the city's mixture of modernity and ancient history.

History

The town's history begins on the very day Gran Canaria was conquered. Juan Rejón landed on 22 June 1477 in the bay which was later to become the harbour of Puerto de la Luz. Rejón and his troops marched off in a southerly direction. It is said that he met an elderly Guanche woman, who recommended that he pitch camp on a river meadow (*vegueta*) in a grove of palm trees (*las palmas*). The invading army established its headquarters in this very place beneath shady fruit trees and with a flowing river, the Guiniguada, to supply fresh water all the year round. According to legend, the old woman appeared to Juan Rejón in a dream as St Anna. For this reason, the cathedral of Las Palmas is dedicated to Santa Ana in honour of the city's patron saint.

The old quarter of Vegueta has remained the heart of the city, and it is from this point that Las Palmas spreads out in a northerly direction. Today the historic centre of Vegueta is a protected area, and in 1990 it was declared a world heritage site and placed under the special protection of UNESCO.

Las Palmas today has some 500,000 inhabitants and is thus by far the largest town in the Canary Islands. It is also the largest port in the archipelago, the eighth-largest city in Spain and the seat of government of the Autonomous Region of the Canary Islands. The town derives its income largely from service industries; indeed, almost 80 percent of the population makes its living in this way.

Tourism, however, which was initially centred on the island capital, moved its centre of activity some twenty years ago to the south coast of the island (see Route 4). There were once 30,000 hotel beds in Las Palmas, but this figure has shrunk to 17,000 today. Since 1985, some 35

percent of all hotels and apartment complexes have been closed down. The buildings are being put to new uses as council housing or administrative offices; the city administration, for example, now occupies what was formerly the four-star hotel Rocamar.

Plaza de Santa Ana and a coat-of-arms

21

These changing economic fortunes have repeatedly cast a shadow across the town's five centuries of history. Las Palmas became a cathedral city in 1485 and in 1504 the seat of the Inquisition. During its first golden age as the trading centre for sugar cane and African slaves, British and Dutch pirate ships cruised off the coast in order to capture fleets from America or at least to plunder the city's riches. Sir Francis Drake and John Hawkins were both defeated at sea, as was the Dutch buccaneer Pieter van der Does, who nonetheless managed to burn the city down to its foundations in 1599.

The fertile neighbouring islands of La Palma, La Gomera and Tenerife soon overshadowed Gran Canaria and its capital. When Napoleon occupied the Spanish mainland and deposed the king, La Laguna on Tenerife declared itself the capital of the Canary Islands in 1808. Las Palmas experienced a brief boom in 1881, when Fernando León y Castilla, a native of Gran Canaria, was nominated the foreign minister of Spain. He ordered the development of the port in his home town, thus enabling Las Palmas to become the port of disembarkation for emigrants returning from America.

Faded elegance

The rivalry between the two large islands of the archipelago as to which town would become the capital of the group was decided in 1927, but has not been laid to rest to this day. Madrid divided the islands into two provinces, and Las Palmas became the capital of one of them, which included not only Gran Canaria but the neighbouring islands of Lanzarote and Fuerteventura. Even the founding of the Autonomous Region of the Canary Islands in 1982 has not altered the competition between the towns: today the government may sit in Las Palmas, but the parliament meets in Santa Cruz de Tenerife. And yet Las Palmas, by virtue of its population, its port and the the longer history, still claims to be the capital of the Canary Islands.

Walk 1: Narrow streets – broad perspectives

The maze of narrow streets of the ★★★ **Vegueta Old Town** nestles on the west side of the Fuente de Mendoza and Calvo Sotelo motorways. History is omnipresent here. At every turn you will see Andalusian balconies, Moorish

All-round view in the old town

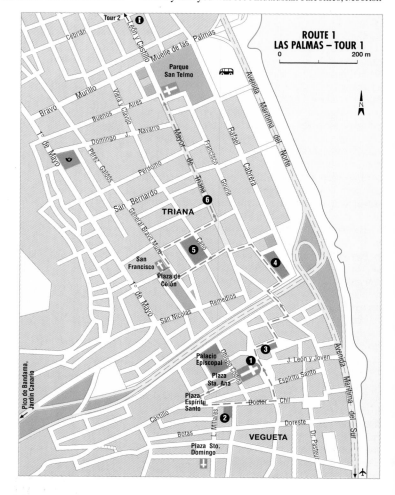

decorative elements on the doorways and even Ionic columns in front of the stately buildings. Tucked in between are *palacios* which look like fortresses, with patios full of brightly coloured flowers in which even holiday makers will forget the city stress back home. The names of the houses read like a 'Who's Who' of Canary Islands history: Morales and Manrique, Alfaro and Padilla.

Dominating the scene is the ★★ **Catedral de Santa Ana ①**. The twin towers of the triple-naved building overshadow the Old Town. Construction work started almost as soon as the Spanish arrived in 1497, but it took almost 400 years to complete, which explains the variety of architectural styles which can be spotted both inside and out: Gothic in the interior at the back of the building and in the chapels along the left aisle, baroque in the San Fernando Chapel, Renaissance in the right aisle and an eclectic mixture in the crossing cupola. The neoclassicism on the facade, like many of the statues inside the cathedral, is the work of the Canary Island sculptor José Luján Pérez (1756–1815).

Catedral de Santa Ana

The **Museo Diocesano del Arte Sacro** (entrance in Calle Espíritu Santo) houses not only church treasures but also booty from former Spanish colonies, including a number of notable Aztec works of art (Monday to Friday 9am–1.30pm, Saturday 9am–2pm).

In front of the cathedral is the main square of the Old Town, the ★ **Plaza Santa Ana**, for more than 500 years the most important square in Las Palmas. Dogs, the town's heraldic animals, stand guard at the entrance to the square, which today is an arena for pigeons, a children's playground and a favourite meeting place for local gossips.

Plaza Santa Ana and a boy's best friend

The square is bordered by the magnificent palaces built for the church dignitaries. All that remains of the **Palacio Episcopal** (Bishop's Palace) is the doorway, lone survivor of the fire which destroyed the town in 1599 following the invasion of the Dutch buccaneer Pieter van der Does. Next door stands the **Casa Regental**, the former residence of the royal governor. On its splendid doorway can be seen the coat of arms of the united kingdoms of León and Castile, which provided the kings of Spain during the 15th and 16th centuries.

Opposite the cathedral is the former **ayuntamiento** (Town Hall). Although it is over 150 years old, it is still the youngest building on the square. The original building was reduced to ashes on Easter Sunday 1842 after the roof truss was hit by a rocket. To this day, the arrival of the Easter holiday is marked by letting off fireworks on the Plaza. Less hazardous, however, is another annual event which takes place here. As part of the Corpus Christi celebrations the square is decked out with a magnificent carpet of flowers.

Morbid display in the Museo Canario

Not far from the Plaza, past the Casa Romero, which once served as primary school for the nearby Jesuit college, you will arrive at the ★★★ **Museo Canario ❷**. This privately-owned museum (Monday to Friday 10am–1pm and 4pm–7.30pm, Saturday 10am–1pm, Sunday 10am–2pm; library Monday to Friday 4–7pm) is the finest museum in the archipelago. It houses the Canary Islands' largest and most up-to-date collection of objects dating from pre-Spanish times and is a must for visitors who are interested in the early history of the islanders. The pottery, tools, mummies and skeletons of the original inhabitants are presented in a series of informative displays. The museum also contains a comprehensive collection of Cro-Magnon skulls. The existence of these relics has repeatedly given rise to speculation as to the origins of the early Canary Islanders. Also on view is a replica of the *Cueva Pintada*, one of the most important early buildings on the islands (*see page 39*).

Another sight which should be included on every visitor's itinerary is ★ **Casa Colón ❸**. It seems doubtful that Christopher Columbus ever really lived in this house, as town historians would have one believe. At any rate, it is certain that he cannot have spent the night here before his first Atlantic crossing. If he ever set foot on the Canary Islands, then the only possible date must have been 25 August 1492, and if so, then in haste and in a bad mood because a broken rudder on the 'Pinta' forced him to alter course. That, at least, is the opinion of a group of experts from the Spanish Admiralty in 1992, with the result that the 500th anniversary of the discovery of America took place without the involvement of the Canary Islands. (It has been proven, however, that Colón, as Columbus is known in Spanish, landed several times on the neighbouring island of La Gomera.)

Casa Colón and detail

Even so, the Casa Colón is worth a visit (Monday to Friday 9am–1.30pm, Saturday 10am–1pm, Sunday 10am–1.30pm; library Monday to Friday 4–8pm). The building was restored about forty years ago, but the richly decorated doorway, the well in the inner courtyard and some parts of the stonework date from the time of the Spanish conquest. The rest of the building complex, which stretches halfway along the street, is made up of houses built over the last three centuries.

The rooms in which the museum is housed have been made to look suitably old. Columbus's various expeditions are presented with great clarity by means of model ships, replicas of maps and various items of equipment. There is also a collection of paintings and sculptures and a library.

Checkmate in Triana

The **Triana** district adjoins the Vegueta. Named after 16th-century Andalusian settlers and bearing the same name as one of the quarters of Seville, it is the oldest shopping and commercial district in Las Palmas. Directly on the main road which divides the two quarters stands the **Teatro de Pérez Galdós ❹**, which is named after the Canary Islands' most famous son, the best-known Spanish novelist of the turn of the century, Benito Pérez Galdós (1843–1920). Opened in 1919, the theatre was built according to the plans of Miguel Martín Fernández de la Torre and decorated by his distinguished brother, Néstor (*see page 27*). Lying a short distance further on at Calle Cano No 6, the house where Galdós was born and spent his early years is today the ★ **Museo Pérez Galdós ❺** (Monday to Friday 9am–1pm; library Monday to Friday 4–8pm). The building is a fine example of Canary Islands architecture, with a picturesque courtyard. It houses the most comprehensive collection of writings by and about Galdós, and is furnished with original items from his house in Madrid. The study, in which a life-size wax model of the writer can be seen sitting at the desk, adds a macabre touch.

Pérez Galdós

Galdós's development as the 'Spanish Balzac' began and ended in Madrid. He wrote more than 100 novels and is one of the most widely read Spanish authors to this day. He was a social critic who gradually changed from anti-clericalism to socialism. Recognition on the international literary scene helped him to achieve a breakthrough in conservative Spain. Today his portrait adorns the 100-Peseta banknote, and one of his most important works, the novel *Nazarin*, was filmed during the 1960s by the grand master of Spanish film, Luis Buñuel. Despite the fact that Galdós left Gran Canaria at the age of 19, never referred to his 'homeland' in his works and returned only once on a brief visit, his native island bears no grudge against him.

The Triana District is almost as old as the Vegueta, but has a much more bustling atmosphere. Crossing it is the **Calle Mayor de Triana** ❻, a granite-paved street which is closed to traffic and which leads past the Parque San Telmo. The latter contains the **Ermita de San Telmo**, a small chapel dedicated to the patron saint of fishermen with a fine coffered ceiling in Mudéjar style. The pedestrian precinct has a sleepy, old-fashioned air, but the shops along here are in fact very fashionable. Calle Mayor de Triana is the most elegant street for shopping and strolling in Las Palmas. Besides jewellers and the inevitable souvenir shops there is a remarkably large number of stores selling electrical goods. Shoe shops offer a range of elegant but inexpensive footwear.

Calle Mayor de Triana

Some of the facades bear witness to the expansion of the area as a business district. Particularly noteworthy are **No 35** and **No 80**, both dating from the second half of the last century. There are also several historic facades revealing the influence of *modernisme*, the Spanish version of art nouveau, in the neighbouring streets (Domingo Navarro and Calle Buenos Aires).

And Christopher Columbus is not far away. A bust of the discoverer of the New World surveys the Plaza Colón to the west of the shopping area. Worth seeing is the **Casa Lezcano** on the left-hand side. The three-storey townhouse is two hundred years old and is decorated with squares of stone framing the main doorway, as well as wooden balconies over two storeys.

Iglesia San Francisco

It is well worth taking a glimpse inside the **Iglesia San Francisco** on the far side of the square. Destroyed in the fire of 1599, the church was rebuilt in stages, the last of which was in 1961. Fortunately the wooden Mudéjar-style ceiling was retained, and the decoration introduced by Moorish craftsmen can still be admired.

Walk 2: City oases

Adjoining the Old Town, which consists of the Vegueta and Triana districts, lie Arenales and Lugo, two quarters which the visitor is advised to ignore. On a level with the yacht harbour, the Muelle Deportivo, you will reach the Ciudad Jardín, a district full of parks and villas dating from the 1920s. Here, too, is the ★ **Parque Doramas** ❼, the city's green lung. The park is named after Doramas, a chief of the Guanches who resisted the invading Spanish until the bitter end. According to legend, Doramas was pierced by the lance of Pedro de Vera while fighting the Spaniard in single combat on Montaña de Arucas (*see page 36*); the Guanche warriors, deprived of their leader, all threw themselves into the barrancos. The monument at the entrance to the park recalls this desperate act.

This urban oasis off Calle León y Castillo is dominated by the luxurious **Hotel Santa Catalina**. Founded in 1890 by the British and built by Manuel Martín Fernandez de la Torre according to the design of his brother, Néstor, it is the oldest five-star hotel on the island and still one of the best addresses in town. Visitors may consider taking a drink on the verandah before continuing with their tour. To the northwest of the hotel lies the largest swimming pool in town, and to the south lie the Pueblo Canario and the Museo Néstor.

Hotel Santa Catalina

27

Built in mock Canary-Island style, the ★ **Pueblo Canario** ❽ or 'Canary-Island Village' was established in 1939 by Miguel Martín Fernández de la Torre, based on an idea of his brother, Néstor. Planned exclusively for tourists, it is a complex of restaurants, handicraft shops (selling everything from embroidered table cloths to Canary knives) and a tourist information office. Don't miss the displays of music and dancing by performers in Canary Islands traditional costumes on Thursdays at 5.30pm and on Sundays at 11.45am. The combination of melancholy Canary-Island songs and passionate *salsa* rhythms introduced by immigrants from the Caribbean is well worth seeing and hearing.

In the Pueblo Canario

In honour of the artist, one of the houses has been turned into the ★ **Museo Néstor** ❾ (Tuesday to Friday 10am–1pm, Thursday also 2–8pm, Saturday 10am–12 noon and 2–8pm, Sunday 11am–2pm). Néstor Martín Fernández de la Torre (1887–1938) was the first Canary Islands artist to achieve international recognition. He is regarded as one of the leading representatives of *modernisme*, and carried out a large number of projects in this style on the mainland as well as on his native island, not least the decoration of the Teatro de Pérez Galdós (*see page 25*).

Erotic scene from Néstor's Poema de la Tierra

As well as a collection of furniture and designs for stage settings, the museum contains a permanent exhibition of

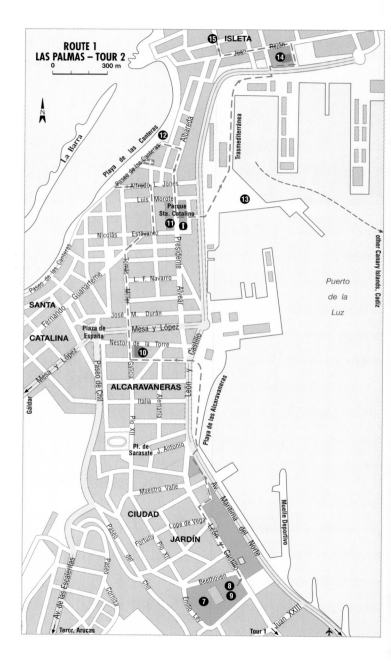

ROUTE 1
LAS PALMAS – TOUR 2

0   300 m

ISLETA

Juan   Rejón

⑮   ⑭

La Barra

Playa de las Canteras

Paseo de las Canteras

Albareda

⑫

Trasmediterránea

Alfredo L. Jones

Luis Morote

Parque
Sta. Catalina

⑪ ⓘ

Nicolás Estévanez

Presidente Alvear

⑬

other Canary Islands, Cadiz

Paseo de las Canteras

28

L. F. Navarro

Jones

Millet

Guanarteme

Fernando

SANTA

Puerto
de la
Luz

José M. Durán

Plaza de
España

Mesa y López

CATALINA

Castillo

Néstor de la Torre

⑩

Mesa y López

Gáldar

Paseo de Chil

Galicia

ALCARAVANERAS

León

Italia

Alemania

Playa de las Alcaravaneras

Pío XII

Pl. de
Sarasate

J. Antonio

Maestro Valle

Av. Marítima del Norte

Muelle Deportivo

CIUDAD

Lope de Vega

Paseo del

Paseo

Fortuny

Pío XII

JARDÍN

León   Castillo

Av. de las Escaleritas

Chil

Cornisa

Beethoven

⑧
⑨

⑦

Emilio Ley

Juan XXIII

Teror, Arucas

Tour 1

Néstor's most famous paintings. Amongst his favourite themes were the countryside of his native island as well as the plants and animals to be found there. Néstor's most important works are the picture cycles *Poema del Mar* and *Poema de la Tierra* which contain the recurring themes of earth, people, animals and the waves of the Atlantic.

Bordering this miniature garden city is the shopping district of **Alcaravaneras**. Those who wish to avoid big-city bustle and noise and exhaust fumes should stick to the east coast and skirt round the district by walking along the dark sandy beach **Playa de las Alcaravaneras**. By taking this route you will also arrive in due course at the **Avenida Mesa y López**, where branches of the Spanish department stores 'El Corte Inglés' and 'Galerias' stand side by side with international fashion designers and expensive boutiques. Those who prefer more modest wares should come on Sundays between 10am and 3pm. Traders display their goods on the tree-lined paseo in a lively fleamarket (*rastro*). Exotic fruits, silvery fish and crisp salads will be found on weekdays just round the corner (Calle Galicia) in the covered market, the **Mercado Central ❿**.

Playa de las Alcaravaneras

We have now arrived at the very heart of Las Palmas. Here, where the sea forces the town onto a narrow causeway of land, lies the ★ **Santa Catalina District** and the park of the same name. Apart from the port, this is the main tourist area and yet another shopping centre. The blend is fascinating. Junk shops full of dusty souvenirs from all over the world stand cheek by jowl with others stocked with expensive jewels and furs. There are bazaars stacked high with goods in disordered profusion in which you will find high-quality electrical goods at competitive prices. And in between are countless bars and other drinking establishments which have helped to establish Las Palmas' reputation as the Spanish town with the most pubs.

Muelle de Santa Catalina

Sailors from the nearby port stroll through the streets, black African traders ply their wares, gypsy children sell roast almonds and shoeshine boys squat in front of their elegantly dressed clients. Here, in Catalina, Las Palmas shows itself to be a cosmopolitan harbour town and a metropolis free of tourist crowds.

The narrow streets lead straight up towards the ★★ **Parque Santa Catalina ⓫**, the liveliest square in town. At any hour of day or night, everyone gathers here, be they early birds or night owls. Businessmen in the morning to swallow a quick *cafecito* instead of breakfast, tourists from the hotels bordering the nearby Canteras Beach arrive on a sightseeing trip at about ten, and towards noon you will see workers from the neighbouring offices grabbing a *tapa*. After lunch, elegantly dressed ladies recover from a shopping expedition, and in the evenings local lovers

Playa de las Canteras

and sailors from the port take over. And in between them all are the street hawkers and the multilingual waiters, the people selling lottery tickets and the shoeshine boys – and unfortunately the odd pickpocket. Purchasing a lottery ticket may not be worthwhile, but tourists might consider letting Pablo or Carlos earn a little money by cleaning their shoes.

The park is not really a proper park, but rather a magnificent plaza with a few areas of green and a multitude of outdoor cafés. The holidaymakers who come on a sightseeing trip from Maspalomas only play a supporting role.

From the park it is just a short walk to the Paseo de las Canteras, the beach front promenade. On the golden sands of the ★ **Playa de las Canteras** ⓬ , it is hard to distinguish between the sunbathing schoolgirls, the office workers enjoying their midday break and the tourists. The remarkable feature of this beach lies a few hundred metres offshore in the warm waters of the Atlantic, which is still clean at this point: **La Barra**, 'The Barrier'. The reef is 2.5km (1½ miles) long and transforms the sea into a vast natural lagoon – the largest swimming pool in the world, so to speak. Surfers, with or without surfboard, will find amusement at best at the southern end of the beach, where the waves roll unbroken onto the sand.

The Playa de las Canteras is a refuge for town holidaymakers. Side by side along the seafront stand elegant hotels and apartment complexes, some of which have seen better days. The traffic-free promenade is 5km (3 miles) long and serves as a buffer between the bustle of town and the beach idyll. Its numerous little oases of palm trees provide space for bars and cafés, discotheques and restaurants, from the rough-and-ready fisherman's tavern to Chinese or the gourmet Italian, there is somewhere to suit every taste. You will even find the often derided

Apartments line the beach

German beer cellar and Austrian coffee-house. The wide strip of beach is dotted with deckchairs, pedalos and every type of water sports equipment for hire. Lifeguards watch over the 'bathtub', making it an ideal beach even for families with small children.

Even without taking a *tartana*, the popular horse-drawn carriage, it will not take you long to reach the other side of the peninsula, here at its narrowest point. On the other side lies the **Puerto de la Luz** . The 'Harbour of Light' was created at the turn of the century as a vast job-creation project. Today it is the largest port in Spain, but it is struggling to retain its supremacy as a number of African ports compete for Puerto de la Luz's pre-eminent position as the turntable for sea traffic between three continents (Europe, Africa and America).

The 'Harbour of Light'

The harbour of Las Palmas is still important as a tourist port as it serves as the hub for all the main ferry links between the islands of the archipelago. It is also a favourite starting point for amateur sailors, who set out from here to cross the Atlantic. Las Palmas represents the final port for taking on supplies before the long haul westwards. Frequent visitors in winter are the stylish yachts which ferry student crew members across to the Caribbean.

31

And yet, the 'Harbour of Light' is gradually losing a number of its former essential functions. For some years now the cruise ships of the Cunard Line have ceased to tie up at the Muelle Reina Sofia, heading instead for the port of Los Mármoles on Lanzarote. The Las Palmas fishing fleet is still the largest in Spain, but Moroccan fishermen can fish the Sahara Bank much more cheaply than their Canary Islands colleagues. This in turn affects the fish processing industries of Las Palmas. During the 1930s there were 27 factories; today only one survives. The Russian and Korean fishing fleets, which until recently have used Puerto de la Luz as their Atlantic base, have both moved to Dakar in Senegal. The Chinese fleet has recently arrived, however, so the taste of Asia in and around the port will continue to be very much in evidence. The era of Las Palmas as a naval base, the eighth-largest in Spain, is coming to an end. The end of the Cold War has meant that an Atlantic headquarters for the Spanish Admiralty is no longer of vital importance.

Meanwhile, the authorities in Las Palmas are pondering all kinds of schemes to revitalise the port area. If it is allowed to rely solely on the custom of tankers bringing oil, freighters carrying agricultural produce and luxury yachts belonging to millionaires, the port will surely decline still further. Among suggested schemes for the future is the construction of an offshore trading centre situated out in the harbour, an attempt to establish an artificial free trade zone after the Canary Islands lost this cherished status at the end of 1995.

Continuing along the harbour promenade towards Isleta, the northernmost residential district in town, you will come to the **Castillo de la Luz** ⑭. Built during the 16th century, as can be recognised from the Gothic framework surrounding the doorway, the fort once served to defend the town and harbour from marauding pirates, who posed a threat to life and trade. The 'Castle of Light' has recently been renovated and is now the home of a drama school. It can be seen from the outside, but is no longer open to the public. Instead, if you arrive during the late afternoon you can watch the local men playing *boule* in the castle park.

Castillo de la Luz

The climax of the walk is the panoramic view from the highest point of the **Isleta** ⑮. The highest peak (239m/765ft) is visible from afar on the northern edge of town. The steep climb to the top is recommended only for enthusiastic walkers; most other visitors will prefer to take a taxi. From the top of the cliff, under a wooden cross which is larger than a man, you will have a majestic view of the town, harbour and sea.

Excursion

After the beach and sightseeing routine of Las Palmas, many visitors may welcome the combination of peace and fresh air, together with the rich variety of the island's botanical species. The ★★ **Jardín Canario** (daily 9am–6pm) lies in the hamlet of La Calzada near Tafira Alta, an elegant villa suburb 8km (5 miles) southwest of Las Palmas. Those coming by car should take the road towards Tafira Alta, take a fork to the right at the junction in the suburb itself and continue for a short distance along the

The kiosko in Parque San Telmo

minor road in the direction of Las Palmas. The entrance to the Jardín Canario is just a few yards further on. Bus No 58, which runs every hour from the central bus station at Parque San Telmo, stops directly by the main entrance to the gardens; remember to tell the driver that you wish to get out here, however, as he will not stop unless you do so.

Here you will not find the imported exotic flowers which adorn the gardens of expensive hotels, but mostly species which grow only in the Canary Islands, and in some cases not even on all the islands.

Immediately past the main entrance stands a *laurisilva.* (bay laurel). Bay laurel forest is only found extensively today on the Canary Islands of La Gomera and La Palma, and on the Cape Verde Islands, the Azores and Madeira. Five hundred years ago, however, before the Spanish Conquest, Gran Canaria was also covered with cool, damp forest of this kind. Axes and chain saws have long since destroyed the island's native forests. A few paces further on, the garden represents a completely different type of vegetation. Cacti and euphorbias, which thrive in the drier, more low-lying regions of the island, extend their prickly branches high into the clear blue sky.

The garden, which was established in 1952 by the Swedish botanist Eric R. Sventenius, is laid out along the steeply sloping side of a gorge. The differences in height allow for a natural representation of the various climatic zones of Gran Canaria and the typical plants and flowers for each type. Pines and cedars grow happily here beside marguerites, which occur in a number of variations on the island. Amidst a riot of blossom, Jupiter's beard grows directly out of the rocks, and above them all the endemic dragon tree stands sentinel, known throughout the Canary Islands as *drago*.

It is understandable that in the face of so many rare plants, an amateur botanist may be tempted to try to cultivate some of them himself back home. In the interests of environmental protection, however, you should resist the temptation to dig up or break off any of the plants. It is, moreover, strictly prohibited. Many garden centres offer seeds and seedlings which can be purchased and taken home. Even the visitor in a hurry can purchase Canary Island seeds or perhaps a little dragon tree in one of the shops at the airport before departure.

All sections of the garden can be reached by means of narrow paths, some of them fairly steep. They lead past waterfalls and cross a river at one point. The variety of natural settings is as remarkable as the richness of the plant life on this small island, and the barrenness of the landscape today will arouse feelings of sadness that this miniature paradise has been destroyed for ever.

Jardín Canario

The Canary date-palm

Route 2

The north: under the female donkey's belly

Las Palmas – Teror – Agaete – Las Palmas (135km/ 84 miles)

On the road to Teror

The north is still the greenest region of the island, and it is the most important agricultural area. The fertility of the soil stems from the clouds borne by the trade winds which bank up here in front of the central massif, bringing not only shade but also moisture. The average rainfall of 1,000mm (39 inches) per year means that this part of the island receives more rain than some areas of the British Isles. Nonetheless, the precipitation is not sufficient to grow tropical fruits, such as bananas, without irrigation. Agricultural alternatives are thus few and far between. Since the water required for the plants can now be more profitably used for tourism, about one third of the banana plantations have been ploughed up in recent years. The result is that large tracts of land which were once fertile now lie fallow and are turning to scrub.

34

Gran Canaria's famous blue skies are more often obscured by clouds in the north of the island than in other regions. The area has thus acquired the comic nickname of 'La Panza de la Burra', the 'Female Donkey's Belly'. The origins of the name can be explained as follows: in

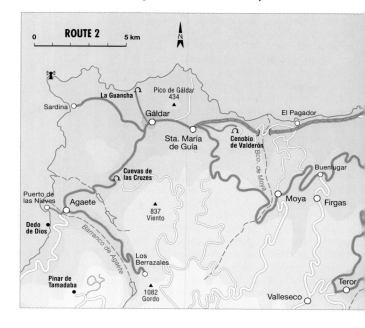

former times, a farmer would look for a shady place in which to spend the midday siesta. If there was no tree available he would lie down beneath a female donkey; a male animal might kick him. When he looked up after his rest, he would see the grey shadow of the donkey's belly, bearing a strong resemblance to the trade-wind clouds.

The first section of the route leads into the island interior, leaving Las Palmas in a south-westerly direction along the C813. Past Tamaraceite, a Guanche word meaning 'Grove of Palm Trees', turn off onto the C817, which winds its way through a series of sharp bends to ★★ **Teror** (11,000 inhabitants), a jewel of Canary Islands architecture, where distinguished townhouses with elaborately carved window surrounds, doors and balconies have been well preserved.

Teror – an architectural jewel

Teror is Gran Canaria's principal religious centre and is the home of the 'Virgen del Pino', the island's patron saint. The miracle-working 'Madonna of the Pine Tree' is said to have appeared to the local inhabitants on 8 September 1481 in a pine tree. The little town boasts a number of lovely churches dedicated to the Virgin Mary. In the centre stands the 18th-century **basilica** in which the patron saint is displayed in sumptuous array, with jewellery, clothing and votive gifts (Monday to Saturday 2–4pm, Sundays and public holidays 10.30am–2pm and 3.30–6pm). The Virgin of the Pine Tree is deeply revered to this

The basilica is dedicated to the Virgin Mary

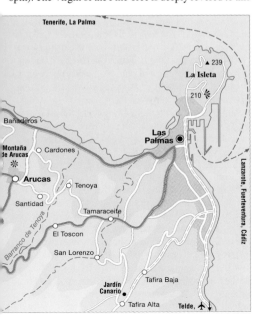

The centre is closed to vehicles

Plaza Teresa de Bolívar, detail

day, and pilgrims flock to Teror all the year round, but especially on her festival day, 8 September.

In front of the basilica in the direction of the entrance to the town stands the former **Bishop's Palace**, in which a cultural centre has been established.

Teror is closed to motor vehicles, which enables visitors to enjoy the traditional Canary Islands atmosphere. Many alleys are cobbled and open up onto little squares, such as the **Plaza Teresa de Bolívar**. The name recalls the wife of the South American freedom fighter and founder of Bolivia, who originally emigrated to Venezuela from Teror. A generation earlier, Simón Bolivar's family had left war-torn Tenerife to seek its fortune in South America, as did many Canary Islanders before and afterwards.

Also worth visiting is the **Finca Osorio** on the outskirts of Teror. Here the Office of Environmental Protection has supported a reforestation project involving the rare laurel trees which once covered the island.

A busy market is held in Teror every Sunday morning. Goods for sale include not only fruit, vegetables and local cheeses, but also clothing and household articles.

Continuing along Road C814, which turns away towards the north, ★ **Arucas** (30,000 inhabitants) soon appears in the distance, the third-largest town on the island. It is dominated on the northern side by the **Montaña de Arucas** (402m/1,286ft), which by means of an approach road and restaurant has been turned into an observation point. The black towers of the cathedral can be seen from afar.

There used to be an abundance of water in and around Arucas. At one time there was even a freshwater lake, so the area offered ideal conditions for the colonisers from Spain to cultivate sugar cane. A number of rum distilleries were also established. The laurel trees that were in the

Arucas from the mountain

neighbourhood were felled to provide fuel. This first round of deforestation was one of the principal reasons for the catastrophic water shortage on Gran Canaria. Arucas is still famous for its rum production today, although the raw materials are now imported. The harvest from the tiny fields on which sugar cane is still grown is barely sufficient to supply even local demand.

As is the case with the whole of the northern part of the island, Arucas fell victim more than once to the problems of single-crop farming. The most recent example was the water-intensive banana plantations. Today, no more than 20 percent of the original area remains under cultivation; stiff competition from Central America has led to a sharp decline in demand. It is clear, however, how lucrative banana farming must have been for at least some of the local inhabitants from the vast size of the church. Built of black lavastone, the gigantic **Iglesia de San Juan Bautista** was begun in 1909 and first used for worship in 1917, but the project remains unfinished to this day. It was supposedly an imitation of the Cathedral of the Holy Family (Catedrale de la Sagrada Família) in Barcelona, designed by the famous modernist architect Antonio Gaudí, another unfinished construction. The most important work of art is the 'Resting Christ' by the Canary Island sculptor Manuel Ramos. Apart from a visit to the church, it is also worth strolling through the **Old Town** of Arucas, which was placed under a protection order in 1979, and through the manicured Parque Municipal, a small botanic garden. In a square in front of the entrance to the park is a monument commemorating the last Canarian chief, Doramas, who is said to have met his end at the hands of the Spanish conqueror, Pedro de Vera, in 1491 (*see page 27*).

Iglesia de San Juan Bautista

37

Leaving the town on the C814, after 6km (4 miles) turn left in Buenlugar towards **Firgas**, a town of modest whitewashed houses on the slopes of a hill, famous for its mineral water. The springs lie in the Las Madres Gorge (15km/9 miles) and the product is widely available on all the Canary Islands. The road through Moya passes picturesque gorges and runs past the last 'wild' laurels in the area, which stretch along the valley floor. Access to the forest itself is now forbidden.

Continuing through **Santa María de Guía**, which is famous for its pottery, the next place on the route is ★★ **Cenobio de Valerón.** To date this is the only archaeological site on the island which has facilities for welcoming visitors. Some 300 caves hollowed out of the volcanic rock were for many years thought to have been a convent complex inhabited by the *Harimaguadas*, the vestal virgins of the Canary Islands who watched over the

Cenobio de Valerón

corn supplies (*cenobio* = convent). Scientists now believe that the caves were merely used as granaries; their remoteness and elevated position made them easy to defend.

The caves, on several levels, are partly natural and partly man-made, hewn by the Guanches from the soft volcanic tufa. At one time they were closed by wooden doors and linked to one another by passages and flights of steps. The complex is reached by a staircase, but can only be viewed from the outside because of the danger of rockfalls. The guard at the entrance makes it quite clear by pointing energetically at a 2,000 peseta note the size of gratuity he considers appropriate (weekdays 9am–1pm and 3–5pm, although the opening times may vary according to the whim of the guard).

On a hill above the site lay a *tagoror*, a place of assembly of the Guanches. Remains of stone benches can still be seen.

Plaza de Santiago, Gáldar

★ **Gáldar** (19,000 inhabitants), a few minutes' drive further on, is proud of its Spanish and pre-Spanish past. Its other name, 'Ciudad de los Guanartemes', means 'City of Rulers'; the town's administrators, however, have done little to exploit the rich legacy of their colourful past. A well-planned development of the pre-Spanish sites in the vicinity could make Gáldar into an interesting tourist destination. Instead, the town looks back wistfully to its golden years as a centre of the banana-growing industry and dreams of constructing a large tourist complex on the as yet undeveloped coast. The decline in banana farming has caused a great deal of unemployment locally.

Before the Spanish conquest, Gáldar was the seat of one of the two chiefs of Gran Canaria, whose palace is believed to have occupied the site of the present-day Iglesia Santiago de los Caballeros. The town itself was founded in

1484 and was the capital of Gran Canaria before Las Palmas. A marble plaque set in the wall of the church proclaims that one day the town would like to rise to this glorious position once more.

By the entrance to the town, in the midst of the confusion of traffic, stands a tall, narrow sculpture representing three Guanche princesses. There is another sculpture in the town depicting Tenesor Semidan, the last of the Guanche chiefs, who collaborated with the Spanish colonisers after being forcibly baptised, and persuaded his people to surrender and accept Christianity. Almost all the names of the streets and squares hark back to the town's pre-Spanish past.

At first sight Gáldar does not seem a very inviting place. However, once you have reached the quiet square in front of the church of **Santiago de los Caballeros** with its shady laurel trees, and if the barkeepers have put out a few chairs and tables, you will enjoy the opportunity for a short rest. The church itself was completed in 1872 after a building period of almost 70 years. Just to the right of the entrance, the font, now framed in wood, is thought to have been shipped over from Andalusia in the late 15th century and used in the baptism of the local populace. The church also contains a number of statues of saints attributed to the sculptor Luján Pérez.

Here, too, is the old **Town Hall**, an old Canaries' building. The crown of the spreading dragon tree in the inner courtyard, claimed to be the oldest on the entire archipelago, rises above the roof of the building. It was planted in 1719, and there seems little room left for it to grow in any direction but upwards (Town Hall open on weekdays, mornings only).

The **Cueva Pintada** ('Painted Cave'), in the centre of town, is another relic from Guanche times. It is considered to be the most valuable discovery of all, for it is the only place on the islands where the cave walls have been decorated with coloured geometrical patterns – squares, triangles and concentric circles. The cave is thought to have had a religious function. For many years, however, the 3-m (10-ft) high cave has not been open to the public. Damp from a nearby banana plantation has badly damaged the paintings and it was decided to close the complex to avoid further damage. An accurate replica of the cave can be seen in Las Palmas in the Museo Canario (*see page 24*), and a number of important exhibits are displayed in the Town Hall in Gáldar. In the meantime, renovations are in progress and it is hoped that the archaeological site can be re-opened to the public in 1996.

The route continues towards **Sardina**, where a miniature resort has been established on the beach protected by

A local of the town

39

Sardina

volcanic rocks. The rustic harbour tavern 'La Fragata' is a good place for a snack, and there are a number of good fish restaurants. **Reptilandia** is a reptile zoo in which the animals on display are kept in relatively natural surroundings. Spiders, snakes and crocodiles can be observed behind protective glass panels (daily 11am–4.30pm).

In order to reach **La Guancha**, which offers further evidence of the life of the original Canary Island inhabitants, you should turn off towards El Agujero on the way back from Sardina to Gáldar. Near the coast lie the remains of a pre-Spanish settlement and necropolis. The site is fenced off and can thus only be observed from a distance. It consists of a circular structure of stones laid without mortar, with two round burial chambers in the centre surrounded by many smaller rectangular chambers. When the site was excavated in 1935, 30 mummies dating from the 11th century were found. It has been suggested that this was the burial place of Canarian Guanche nobles, and that the royal family may have occupied the circular chambers.

The coastal villages in this area contain large numbers of cave dwellings, many of them still in use or even inhabited to this day. Such dwellings can usually be recognised only at second sight, for the present occupiers have constructed facades in front of entrances, making them look like normal houses.

It is easy to miss the **Cuevas de las Cruzes**, the 'Caverns of the Cross'. The site lies on a bend a few yards off the road from Gáldar to Agaete. There is no signpost, nor is there a fence to draw your attention to the caverns, which can be explored at your own risk (take a torch).

The little town of ★ **Agaete** (5,700 inhabitants) stands at the entrance to the most dramatic gorge on Gran Canaria. Its quaint whitewashed houses with wooden balconies remind the visitor of many a small town in Andalusia. In the centre stands the **Iglesia de la Concepción**, which has a fine 16th-century Flemish triptych. Near the church, along Calle Huertas lies the Huerto de las Flores, a small garden containing some fine specimens of Canarian and tropical flowers. Narrow alleys lead away from the square in front of the church into the green, fertile gorge.

Barranco de Agaete

Although the ★★ **Barranco de Agaete** does not lie directly on the route, a detour into this picturesque valley should not be missed. The *barranco* ('gorge') is also often signposted as *valle* ('valley'). Along the roadside lie several restaurants with terraces from which to enjoy the view. Visitors familiar with the neighbouring island of La Gomera will be reminded of the famous 'Valle Gran Rey'. Here, too, you will find tiny terraced fields clinging to the steep sides of the valley which has thus been transformed into a miniature tropical paradise.

Whitewashed cottages are clad with luxuriant bougainvillaea in shades of lilac and red, and on the little fruit plantations grow all the fruits of the earth: lofty papaya trees along the river bed, beside bananas, avocados, oranges, mandarins, mangoes and lemons. Even coffee grows on the higher terraces. Towering in between are the lofty palm fronds of the Canary date palm. At the very top, on the cliffs, grows the Canary pine, with its needles up to 30cm (12in) long and its orange-yellow fruits.

There are mineral springs in the upper section of the *barranco*; the water is bottled and sold. The spa amenities in the little village of **Los Berrazales** were once very popular, but in recent years they have fallen into disrepair.

Fisherman at Puerto de las Nieves

The landscape surrounding the little fishing village of ★★ **Puerto de las Nieves** is romantic in an untamed manner, even dramatic in places. The 'Harbour of Snows' lies near Agaete on the coast, which along this section drops several hundred metres steeply down to the sea. The village's name is less unusual on the Canary Islands than it appears as is not derived from the lofty cliffs, on which snow seldom falls. It refers to the chapel of the Virgen de las Nieves, the 'Madonna of the Snows', who is the patron saint of fishermen.

41

Ermita de las Nieves

The chapel, known as the **Ermita de las Nieves**, looks like a doll's house when compared with the massive sacred buildings elsewhere on the island. During the month of August it houses a jewel of Flemish art: a 16th-century triptych by Joos van Cleve. For the rest of the year the painting is kept in the church of Agaete. The choir also dates from the 16th century, but the nave is 200 years younger. Both, however, are adorned with remarkable Mudéjar carvings. The key for the church can be obtained from Antonio, who lives in house No 2 opposite the chapel.

The waterfront

In the past Puerto de las Nieves was a port of some consequence. The agricultural produce of the whole Agaete area was shipped from here and vessels sailing between Las Palmas and Santa Cruz on Tenerife used to call in. Such bustling activity has long ceased however, leaving just the red and blue fishing cutters to bob up and down beside the new mole. The village contains no high-rise buildings or nondescript modern houses. The single-storey whitewashed fisherman's cottages have brightly painted windows and doors. Along the promenade linking the beach with the harbour lie a number of rustic fishing taverns. Camels and donkeys with saddles wait patiently for little riders.

Restaurant on the beach

The village only really comes alive at weekends, however, when the residents of Las Palmas drive the 60-odd kilometres (38 miles) to enjoy the atmosphere and the fresh fish. From Monday to Friday life moves at a comfortable pace, which appeals to holidaymakers as much as it disturbs the local inhabitants. What the visitors see as a natural idyll represents for those who live here economic ruin. The fishermen's wives may still sell the catch directly out of tin tubs by the roadside, but of the several hundred fishermen who once plied their trade here, only 50 remain, and even for them it is hard to make a living. More than one-third of the residents of Puerto de las Nieves are now without a job. Instead of the attractive peace, the locals would prefer *urbanización*, which in these parts means the development of a region with complexes of holiday flats which bring in their wake new jobs, tourists and money. So far, however, the plans have been opposed by the environmentalists. And yet, for a while now, work has been under way in the harbour. A new mole and a number of smart blocks of flats have already been completed.

Bajada de la Rama in full swing

The fishing village is famous for a festival celebrated with great enthusiasm by locals and visitors alike. Each year on 4 August, the residents of Agaete and Puerto de las Nieves gather fresh branches from the mountains for the 'Bajada de la Rama' ('Procession of the Branches'). Accompanied by traditional dances they carry the branches to the harbour and whip the waves. It is a ritual of pagan origin and is supposed to bring rain and fertility.

Dedo de Dios

To the south of the village the ★★ **Dedo de Dios** is a prominent, bizarrely shaped pinnacle of rock rising from the sea. The 'Finger of God' is such a favourite motive for amateur photographers that it has almost become a symbol of Gran Canaria.

The last leg of the journey, which has followed mostly winding roads, continues now without stopping along the coast road via Bañaderos and Bahía de El Rincón back to Las Palmas.

Route 3

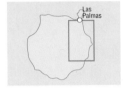
Caldera de Bandama

The east: a look behind the scenes

Las Palmas – Caldera de Bandama – Telde – Las Palmas (90km/ 56 miles) *See map on page 44*

Most visitors get to know this stretch of road immediately after their arrival on the island. Travelling along the east-coast motorway between Gando airport and Las Palmas in the north or the tourist centre of the Costa Canaria in the south, their gaze falls on barren piles of scree, dried-out river beds, industrial complexes and, in the distance, the plastic sheeting covering plantations of tomatoes, cucumbers or cut flowers. Most are horrified: so this is the holiday paradise of Gran Canaria? If, however, they look westwards towards the mountains, they will see how a dry, stony stream bed broadens out into a dramatic palm-fringed gorge. Many a village which at first sight looks uninviting may turn out to harbour remarkable cultural jewels. Well preserved cave dwellings tell of the ancient civilisation of the original Canary Islanders. So take a look behind the scenes and experience an authentic piece of Gran Canaria.

Leaving Las Palmas on the southwest arterial road in the direction of Santa Brígida, the C811 leads past Tafira Alta and the Jardín Canario (*see pages 32–3*) straight to the ★★ **Caldera de Bandama**. The crater, which is 1km (⅝ mile) wide and 200m (650ft) deep, is one of the few places on the island where the volcanic origins of Gran Canaria can be clearly seen. The best view is from the volcanic peak next door, the **Pico de Bandama** (574m/1,883ft), which can be reached by car and has an observation platform and small bar.

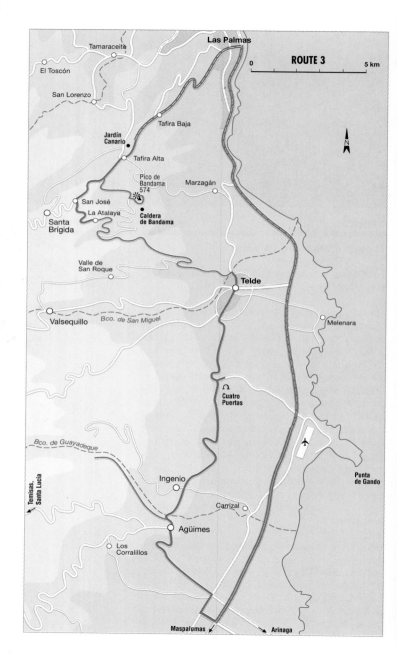

ROUTE 3

0   5 km

Las Palmas

Tamaraceite

El Toscón

San Lorenzo

Tafira Baja

Jardín
Canario

Tafira Alta

Pico de
Bandama
574

Marzagán

San José

La Atalaya

Caldera
de Bandama

Santa
Brígida

Valle de
San Roque

Telde

Valsequillo

Bco. de San Miguel

Melenara

Cuatro
Puertas

Bco. de Guayadeque

Ingenio

Punta
de Gando

Carrizal

Temisas,
Santa Lucía

Agüimes

Los
Corralillos

Maspalomas

Arinaga

More adventurous visitors can spend about 30 minutes climbing down into the crater itself via a steep path which is clearly visible from the rim. There you will find an old, abandoned farmhouse in the shade of two enormous eucalyptus trees, and it is possible to make out the outline of a number of fields which are now lying fallow. In the walls of the craters are cave dwellings which were once the homes of the original Canary Islanders – the Guanches. To reach them, after about five minutes into the descent, turn along a path forking to the left and they're another five minutes away.

The observation platform provides a magnificent view of the whole of the north and east coasts of the island. The towns of Telde and Las Palmas and the surrounding high-rise buildings are in marked contrast to the luxuriant gardens surrounding the villas of the exclusive suburb of Santa Brígida. On a clear day it is sometimes even possible to see the neighbouring island of Fuerteventura to the northeast, whilst the view to the west gives a foretaste of the scenic beauty of the central massif.

The view of Las Palmas

South of the caldera, Spanish for 'cauldron' and the international geological term for a volcanic crater, lies the largest and oldest golf course on Gran Canaria. Visitors who wish to spend their holiday on the fairways will find the **Hotel Golf Bandama** a suitable place to stay in the vicinity (*see page 95*).

Continuing southwards for a short distance along the C811, turn left at San José along the picturesque country road to **Telde** (82,000 inhabitants). At first sight, the second-largest town on the island looks like a modern industrial development. However, the church of St Gregory, the first sight on entering the town, hints at Telde's other character. The town was always an agricultural centre, and the town council still holds a large cattle market during the second and third weeks of November. There are prizes not only for the biggest bull and the best-looking cow, but also for the nicest dog.

A local herdsman

That Telde can look back on a long history becomes evident in San Juan, the northern part of town surrounding the **Iglesia de San Juan Bautista**. The entire district has remained almost entirely free of modern development and has been a protected area since 1981. The plaza in front of the church of St John the Baptist is particularly attractive, as it is surrounded by well preserved and lovingly restored houses in Canary style.

San Juan Bautista

The building of the church itself commenced in 1519, although the towers were added at a much later date. The church houses a precious ★ **Flemish altarpiece** which has been integrated into a baroque setting. The six scenes from the life of the Virgin are regarded as the most valuable

work of Canary art. The vast wealth resulting from the sugar-cane plantations and later from the slave trade introduced by the Spanish colonisers made possible the acquisition of this treasure in 1515. Because of its great value the church is officially only open for services and groups of visitors, but the key can be obtained at any time in the priest's house next door.

The large building on the left-hand side of the square, however, is always open. When planning the new communications centre the architects revived the traditional Canary Islands style of building around a central courtyard. On the street stands the **Casa del Conde de la Vega Grande**. Towards the end of the 1960s the count, whose family greatly influenced the development of Gran Canaria across the centuries, began to transform his uneconomic estates in the south of the island by means of the largest tourist development project in the Canary Islands. The result is the biggest holiday complex in Europe, which has also earned the Count a few millions (*see page 49*).

Another influential island family also came from Telde. The brothers Juan and Fernando León y Castillo both contributed considerably to the economic development of the island during the 19th and early 20th centuries. Fernando became, among other things, the Foreign Minister of Spain, whilst Juan was an engineer and directed the construction of the Puerto de la Luz, the port of Las Palmas. On each of the seven islands in the archipelago you will find at least one street named after the illustrious brothers. Their home town has even dedicated a **museum** to them; it is located, naturally enough, in the Calle León y Castillo 43 (Monday to Friday 9am–9pm, Saturday 10am–1pm).

The history of Telde, however, goes much further back than this. The belief that the legendary Guanche chief Doramas lived here may belong in the realm of myth, but

POLICIA
LOCAL

there is no doubt that the region surrounding Telde was one of the principal settlements of the original islanders. Two of the largest Guanche settlements reputedly lay in the Barranco de Telde: Tara in the north and Cendro in the south. Excavations in Tara unearthed the most important pre-Spanish sculpture on the island: the **Idolo de Tara**, the so-called 'First Mother'. Today it is on view in the Museo Canario in Las Palmas (*see page 24*). Reports dating from the 16th century by the Italian military engineer Leonardo Torriani, who was commissioned by the King of Spain to fortify the Canary Islands against pirate attack, relate that there were 14,000 dwellings in huts and caves.

It is possible to drive out to the site of the settlement where the original inhabitants of Gran Canaria once dwelt. It lies on the western edge of the town near the junction of the road to Valsequillo (on some maps the valley is shown as the Barranco de San Miguel). It is hardly worth doing so, however, as the area has not been fenced off and is now used as an illegal rubbish dump and home for goats.

To be recommended, on the other hand, is a visit to the ★ **Montaña de las Cuatro Puertas** ('Hill of the Four Gates, 319m/1,047ft). It is easily accessible and lies on the C816, the road which leads southwards from Telde to Ingenio. Shortly after the turn-off to the C812, which leads to the airport, a track to the left leads almost to the summit. Here there is a chamber with four entrances (hence the name of the hill), which is believed to have been a cult place of the Guanches. Hollows and gullies in the stones indicate the existence of a place of sacrifice. The open space in front of the cave was a *tagoror*, a place of assembly. Some distance away, on the south side of the hill, are some cave dwellings and storage places.

The two villages further along the C816 from Telde, Ingenio (8km/5 miles) and Agüimes (2km/1½ miles), are not particularly attractive places, but **Ingenio** at least is worth a stopover. Here, during the 16th century, stood huge sugar presses. In South American Spanish, 'ingenio' means 'sugar factory'; in 1991, by the eastern entrance to the town, a monument of a sugar press was set up in memory of better times. Today the little town's only significance is as an embroidery centre, and you will see numerous signs offering 'calados' and 'bordados' for sale. It is worth calling in at the **Museo de Artesania y Piedras**, the Museum for Handicrafts and Rocks (Camino Real de Gando 1), which is mainly a showroom for the sale of Canarian handicrafts and has an embroidery school attached. The collection of rocks has little to offer the non-expert, however, as many of the exhibits are not very well labelled (Monday to Friday 8am–6pm).

Ingenio's sugar press monument

Local lace

Recent attempts to reduce local unemployment have been relatively unsuccessful. The industrial park on the coast near Arinaga was an expensive mistake. With the help of EU subsidies it is now planned to convert the lighthouse **Faro de Arinaga** into a fishing museum, the port to a marina and the two salt flats by the road to the Barranco de Guayadeque to an open-air museum.

Barranco de Guayadeque

The ★★ **Barranco de Guayadeque**, whose steep mountain slopes are honeycombed with cave dwellings, is well worth a detour. Now under a protection order, it is one of the island's most beautiful valleys, where lush and rare Canarian flora still thrives. You need only follow the country road from Agüimes towards Lomo de Caballo into the mountains. The cul-de-sac peters out after some way into a gravel track, but leads into what was the most densely populated gorge on the island during Guanche times. A large quantity of items such as pottery and bones have been recovered from the caves and are now on display in the Museo Canaria in Las Palmas (*see page 24*). Many of the cave dwellings and burial sites are used today as barns or stables. Others are difficult to access because landslides have closed off the entrances. One cave serves as a chapel, in which services are held, and still others are occasionally inhabited by latter-day hippies, despite the regular raids by the Guardia Civil. Visitors wishing to walk right up the valley, beyond the popular **cave-restaurant**, are rewarded by a magnificent view of the mountain landscape.

A cave as a restaurant…

48

The route back to Las Palmas leads through Agüimes again, and from there via a picturesque minor road it is another 6km (4 miles) to rejoin the motorway. Turning left towards Gando, the road continues back to Las Palmas.

…and a cave as a home

Route 4

The south: a mecca for sun-worshippers

Bahía Feliz – San Agustín – Maspalomas – Puerto de Mogán (70km/44 miles)

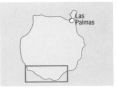

Here it is, Gran Canaria as it appears in the holiday brochures: miles of sandy beaches, bright blue skies, sand dunes and lagoons, crystal-clear Atlantic waters, high-rise hotels and bungalow complexes with luxuriant gardens around elegant swimming pools. In 1995, more than 3 million tourists spent their holidays in Gran Canaria. The south coast already has 200,000 hotel beds and 30,000 more are being built. Apart from the guarantee of fine weather there are plenty of reasons why tourism is booming along the south coast of the island: long beaches to walk along, clean water for bathing, stiff breezes for sailors and surfers, marinas for yacht owners and the 'Holiday World' for harassed parents. Those in search of evening entertainment have a whole variety on offer, and the adventurous can head for the wild gorges of the hinterland. And afterwards everyone can head for the shopping centres, the Wild West towns and the zoos, and can book jeep safaris and pirates' cruises. You will find accommodation and restaurants to suit every pocket: holiday flats in need of a coat of paint and five-star hotels, tapa bars and gourmet temples. The only thing you definitely won't find are lonely beaches.

Where space is at a premium

There is no point in looking for a historic town or even a settlement which has grown up gradually over the years as you drive along the south coast. Apart from the poverty-stricken fishing villages of Arguineguín and Puerto de Mogán, until the 1960s there were no settlements at all along this stretch of the coast. Everything has mushroomed out of the sand in less than one generation; everything was built just for tourists.

This artificial landscape was all derived from the initiative of a single man: the Conde del Castillo de la Vega Grande de Guadelupe. The 'godfather' of Playa del Inglés was the one who saw how to turn his useless estates into a profitable gold mine. In 1962 the first complex was built in San Agustín, and in 1969 began the development of El Oasis Maspalomas and Playa del Inglés. And before long the armies of building workers, by now financed by international tourist companies, moved into every little bay and inlet. The projects were divided into various phases, all tastes were catered to and every kind of holiday dream can be discerned in the architecture of the holiday towns along the coast. Puerto Rico and Bahía Feliz attract sportsmen, San Agustín is for those in search of peace and quiet and El Oasis is for the fashionable. Playa del Inglés is favoured by package tourists, whilst individual holidaymakers might prefer Puerto de Mogán.

The boom lasted for twenty years. Then, towards the end of the 1980s, the growth statistics stagnated. European holidaymakers found the prices too high and the service too poor. Since then the peseta has been devalued three times and the popularity of Gran Canaria has risen again. But the shock has had an effect. At present, attempts are being made to develop a coherent tourist policy. 'Turismo rural', rural tourism, is the watchword, although this is being applied more to the interior of the island than this busy stretch of coast.

Fun for all the family

50

Leaving Las Palmas on the motorway CG1 in a southerly direction, after 40km (25 miles) you will think you have entered another big city. Multi-lane highways and high-rise buildings, with only the odd patch of artificial green in between and seldom an unobstructed view of the beach and the sea – the Costa Canaria is one vast *urbanización*.

The best seaside resorts and most attractive beaches are strung along the coast like a necklace. The first of these is **Bahía Feliz**, the 'Fortunate Bay'. The new development consisting of modern bungalows and apartment hotels was designed for young, dynamic and well-to-do holidaymakers. A paradise for sports enthusiasts has grown up around the Dunkerbeck family's surfing school. The Danish brother and sister Britt and Björn, whose father became a Spanish citizen some years ago, have almost made the world championship in windsurfing their own. Their train-

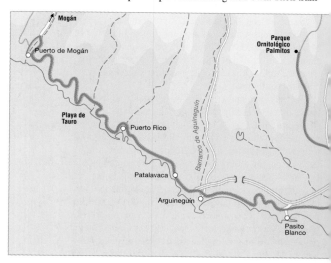

San Agustín

ing ground lies directly opposite their front door, and the regular northeast trade winds make conditions in the bay ideal for practising.

The holiday village at Playa del Aguila, **Nueva Europa**, is not quite as young as the name would have you believe. A relatively small complex consisting of holiday houses with a private, sheltered beach, it was built with visitors in mind who prefer a quiet holiday. That is not to say that there are no restaurants and supermarkets, but for an evening pub crawl you will have to drive to Playa del Inglés, 5km (3 miles) away.

On the way you will pass through **San Agustín**, the heart of the tourist region on the south of the island. The resort was planned from the very start to appeal to the

Playa del Aguila

51

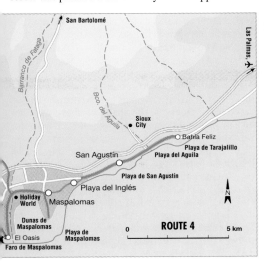

discriminating visitor. This is still obvious, although San Agustín is showing its age now. The 50-odd holiday-flat complexes have spacious, well-kept gardens. The coast road divides the development into two sections – the lower one by the beach and the upper one on the hillside. The latter has better views across the bay. From some places you can even see as far as the white dunes of Maspalomas, although there is a longer walk to the beach. The sandy beach is one of the finest on the island; like most beaches between here and Maspalomas, it is ideal for children. San Agustín can also boast plenty of sports facilities: sailing, golf, riding and much more. Nonetheless, the resort remains relatively quiet.

Playa del Inglés

Playa del Inglés, the largest tourist centre on the south coast, has something to suit every taste and all purses: some 350 bars and restaurants, 250 holiday-flat complexes, 50 discos and 20 large hotels. The main attraction is the long, white-sand beach which extends over 10km (6 miles), with sand dunes reaching to the Maspalomas lighthouse. The scorching-hot beach is so large that even in summer there is plenty of room for the thousands of beachgoers. The only really crowded area is likely to be the water's edge, which can become a bit of a crush.

The resort's history can be seen at a glance. In the middle of the 1960s, high-rise developments were the last word in modernity. Playa del Inglés therefore looks like a dormitory suburb: broad streets, mostly multi-storey buildings, not much greenery and three vast shopping centres as well as a number of smaller ones. The oldest of the three, the Kasbah (Avenida de España), has retained a certain individual charm. The two others, Yumbo and Citá, could be on the outskirts of almost any new town development anywhere in Europe. During the evening they become a favourite place for a stroll, with discos galore and German-style pubs serving meatballs and strawberry gâteau with whipped cream.

Catering to all tastes

Playa del Inglés, even more than the other resorts along the Costa Canaria, is struggling to survive in the face of the economic problems. The number of empty hotels and holiday flats is noticeable even outside the low season, which on Gran Canaria means during the summer months. There are now simply too many rooms available, and although the hoteliers try to make ends meet by offering rock-bottom prices, the local council has decided on an emergency plan which is now being put into effect. It involves a planting programme for the pavements and central islands along the avenidas, the development of the beachfront promenade and the provision of more squares with benches and quiet areas – all designed to make Playa del Inglés more attractive.

Maspalomas lies at the western end of Playa del Inglés. As a resort it is some ten years younger, with a predominance of bungalow complexes and single-storey holiday flats in a garden with pool. In order to set themselves apart from the neighbouring developments, the builders of Maspalomas chose a rustic style with plenty of landscaped open spaces and an 18-hole golf course. The disadvantage lies in the greater distances between the facilities. As the street names indicate, much of Maspalomas was built by German tour operators; you may thus find yourself in Avenida Touropa or TUI, Neckermann or Tjaereborg.

Although the ★★ **Dunes of Maspalomas** are the main attraction along the Costa Canaria, they are often disrespectfully described by the locals as 'the desert'. In fact, the mountains of sand are a spectacular sight. Some of them are tens of metres high and cover an area of 4sq km (1½sq miles). At the far end stands a lighthouse (*faro*) which is 56m (179ft) high and more than 100 years old. The sand dunes have been declared a nature reserve (please keep to the paths); some sections have been allocated for nude bathing.

It is often erroneously claimed that the bright yellow sand was blown across to Gran Canaria from the Sahara. In fact, it originally came from the sea. At one time Gran Canaria was 90m (96yds) wider at this point. The coast was torn away by the sea and then re-deposited along with the dunes. The sand was formed to a large extent from the shells of crustaceans which have been ground to a fine powder by wind and waves.

The beach and dune area can be reached by following the narrow footpath along the **Oasis of Maspalomas**. This grove of palm trees was formerly a haven and breeding place for many bird species. The nature protection laws

Maspalomas lighthouse and dunes

Taking it easy

came too late here too, as in the case of the El Charco lagoon at the estuary of the Barranco de Fataga; the rare species have long since moved on. The main culprit is the small, exclusive tourist development **El Oasis**. Situated directly beside the beach and the sand dunes, the elegant hotels and bungalows tucked away between park-fringed streets are still regarded as the jewel of the entire tourist area.

After so much sand and sun, you may long for a little variety. Excursions can be made to a number of amusement parks in the vicinity. A children's favourite to the northeast of San Agustín is **Sioux City**, which can be reached by following a side road leading up into the mountains from the motorway near Playa del Aguila. Arid, steppe-like vegetation characterises the Barranco del Aquila, the 'Eagles' Gorge'. The very name arouses memories of Buffalo Bill, and the landscape forms an ideal backdrop for the 'Western Show Town' complete with saloon, bank and numerous other buildings which look so authentic that you expect John Wayne to appear any minute. A number of films have been shot in the streets and in front of the dilapidated corral. For the benefit of tourists, bank raids and cattle drives are staged at high noon and 5.30pm. And on Friday evening there is an original Barbecue Night with live country music. (Tuesday to Sunday 10am–8pm, closed Monday.)

Rancho Park is in the middle of Playa del Inglés. You can rent horses, take part in group excursions on horseback or book riding lessons. There is also a good restaurant and a children's playground (daily 10am–10pm).

Holiday World is a vast amusement complex on the way in to Maspalomas. It offers young and young-at-heart local and foreign visitors every imaginable distraction:

Ocean Park

54

scooters, a giant wheel, roundabouts, a big dipper and an open-air dance floor. It adjoins **Ocean Park**, an amusement complex with artificial waves and water slides (Monday to Friday from 5pm, Saturday and Sunday from 3pm).

★★ **Parque Ornitológico Palmitos** is an artificial oasis filled with subtropical plants and covering an area of 200,000sq m (239,000sq yds). It lies some 10km (6 miles) north of Maspalomas and is accessible by public bus as well as being signposted from the motorway. In Playa del Inglés, bus stops are indicated by yellow signs on which the departure times are also listed (approx. every 30 mins). Buses also run from San Agustín and Puerto Rico to the park.

Between steep slopes dotted with wild euphorbias, ponds were dug and 45 species of palm tree planted along with agaves, cacti and orchids. The park has become the habitat for 1,500 birds belonging to more than 200 exotic species. Particular attractions of the little botanical garden are the butterfly house and the parrot demonstrations held seven times daily. There is also a cafeteria and a restaurant (9am–6pm).

A parrot shows off its skills
Pause for refreshment

Continuing in a westerly direction (by now you have passed the southernmost point of Gran Canaria), you will notice the bulky domes and huge antennas of the NASA space centre in Maspalomas. It was from here that the first moon landing by the US astronaut Neil Armstrong was tracked and other Mercury and Apollo missions observed (not open to the public).

Pasito Blanco lies south of the road beside the sea. It owes its significance as a marina to its pretty little bay, which is to be developed into a sports centre.

Arguineguin and **Patalavaca** mark the start of the administrative district of Mogán. Here the landscape also changes. The coast no longer consists of long, white beaches but becomes steep and rocky with numerous small, sheltered bays with darker sand. The airborne sand which can make sunbathing on the eastern beaches unpleasant during periods of 'Africa weather', does not penetrate into these bays, which lie warm and dry in the wind shadow of the northeast trades. Arguineguin, however, which is recognisable from afar because of its cement factory, is no place for holidaymakers. As a town it is uninteresting, its beach polluted and its harbour too dull.

The same really applies to the neighbouring enclave of Patalavaca. Nonetheless, hotel complexes built by luxury chains sprout out of the hillside along the rocky coast. Since they are not high-rises the sea views remain unimpaired. Nor have the investors attempted to economise on the amenities. The cleverly planned schemes more than compensate for the somewhat unattractive location.

Maritime motif

Puerto Rico is the small, sport-loving alternative to Playa del Inglés, which by now is some 20km (13 miles) away. Here, too, there are no high-rises to spoil the view. Instead, the blocks of flats rise up the steep slopes of a gorge which opens onto a semicircular bay with light-coloured sand. The hilliness makes the development tiring for guests, especially as the promised lifts have not yet been built. The harbour is Spain's sailing mecca. Members of the local sailing school have managed to bring home five Olympic gold medals (three from Barcelona and two from Los Angeles). The town council has expressed its thanks for making Puerto Rico famous by naming streets after them.

The most important sport of all here, however, and one which even beginners can indulge in, is deep-sea fishing. For a fat fee, fast boats take groups of four to six anglers out to the well-stocked waters between the islands, where whales, dolphins and – less frequently than would-be heroes would have one believe – even sharks can be seen. The main prize, however, is tuna, especially the *bonito*, a large predator which often appears on the menu in Canary Islands restaurants. Even this apparently sedatory occupation can bring its share of fame and honour: the professionals of Puerto Rico can lay claim to 34 world records in deep-sea fishing.

The town centre can offer little of interest apart from a small park and a vast shopping complex in which the tourist information office is also to be found. Swimming is not exciting here as the bay is protected by moles and the beach created by bringing in lorry-loads of sand. That is probably why Puerto Rico decided to built the longest water slide in the world.

Playa de Tauro is elegant in blue and white with marble everywhere. Individual tourists are also welcome here; the elaborately designed swimming complexes with various pools, waterfalls and suspension bridges are open to the public. They were built by the community for the benefit of hoteliers and their well-to-do customers.

** **Puerto de Mogán**, at the far end of Gran Canaria's southern coastal road, has become a jewel of Gran Canaria's tourist-development policy. Not so long ago, old men gathered to reminisce by the quayside. Today the main road winding through the village has become busy with tourists. Until as recently as the early 1980s, rusty boats bobbed on the waves in the harbour. Once an unassuming little place with a population of only 400, Puerto de Mogán has been transformed into the island's most successful tourist project, and with 2,000 guest beds the development has been kept within reasonable bounds.

The harbour and a pretty square

The local authorities advertise Puerto de Mogán as 'Little Venice'. There are arched bridges spanning the little canals and alleys. Bordering the quay and promenade are welcoming two-storey houses in typical local style with brightly coloured door and window frames and wrought-iron balconies. Vibrant bougainvillaea grows in profusion. The harbour master's headquarters, a four-storey tower in local style, overlooks the picturesque little town. The new harbour juts much further out into the sea, thus creating moorings for almost one hundred sea-going yachts.

No cars are allowed on the little streets and prettily appointed squares, and numerous cafés, bars and restaurants all tempt the visitor to linger. German beers are served, along with German apple cake with whipped cream and redcurrant and raspberry jelly with vanilla ice-cream. Every day, thousands of day trippers from other parts of the island come to wander through the romantic alleys, enjoying the picturesque old-fashioned street lamps and fountains and posing for photographs in front of the luxury sailing yachts. Some of them even venture on a submarine journey through the underwater world. The bright yellow submarine has a glass bottom which permits a fascinating view of the fish and aquatic plants (departures hourly from the harbour of Puerto de Mogán).

The local beach, Playa de Mogán, has been covered in fine, lightly-coloured sand, and a breakwater ensures safe bathing for children. Unfortunately, most visitors fail to find the way to the old centre of the port. This is a shame, as the historic fishing village has also profited from the new prosperity. Along the cobbled streets you will see only freshly painted, sometimes newly plastered cottages. Radio antennas adorn the modern fishing boats in the old harbour. Beyond the wide bay, you will even discover an undeveloped corner of Gran Canaria with old-fashioned farmhouses and dusty paths.

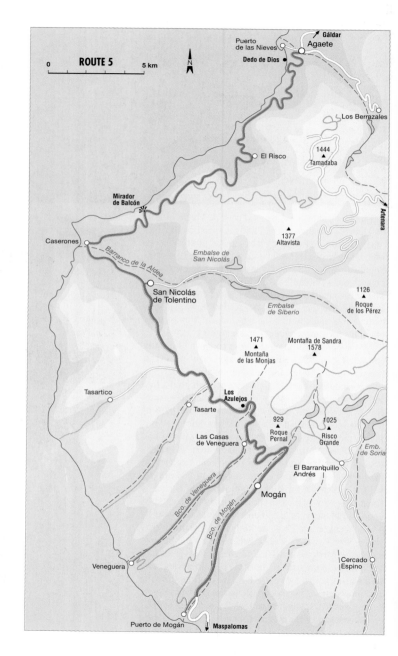

Route 5

The west: unspoilt nature

Puerto de Mogán – Veneguera – San Nicolás de Tolentino – Agaete (90km/56 miles)

Apart from the broad Barranco de San Nicolás de Tolentino and the little village of Veneguera on the coast, the western region of Gran Canaria is virtually uninhabited, and thus appropriately described as the 'Wild West'. Except for a single tongue of land, the beach at Veneguera, the magnificent scenery which ends in the craggy inlets of the steep west coast, has all been declared a conservation area. To the west and south, as far as the eye can see, extends an endless succession of gold, grey and red cliffs. On the slopes of Los Azulejos the green discolouration reveals where the iron in the rocks has been oxidised. On the upper slopes grows the Canary pine, but on the drier lower reaches, the only vegetation consists of the *tabaibas*, which have adapted to the arid climate, euphorbias and the prickly pears, which traditionally provided the food of the cochineal. The few isolated farmhouses are almost all derelict, and the walls supporting the terraced fields have fallen into disrepair.

59

If you have always wanted to hire a jeep, this tour of the lonely mountains of Gran Canaria provides an ideal opportunity. However, even a Seat Panda will be able to cope with the inclines, albeit at a more sedate pace.

The first section of road, which leads from the fashionable holiday resort of Puerto de Mogán (*see page 56*) through the **Barranco de Mogán** into the interior, is still easy territory. The products of this fertile valley are often offered for sale along the roadside: passion fruit, papaya, avocados, mangoes and guavas.

Until the early 1970s, the town of **Mogán**, situated at the upper end of the valley, was nothing more than a remote mountain village. Despite the fact that the community of Mogán covered the largest administrative district on the island, it could only be reached by winding footpaths. Today, a number of artists and other members of the 'alternative' scene have settled here, and, having been discovered by the tourists as well, the place has become very prosperous. Owing to the plentiful supply of water in the valley, the gardens are luxuriant, and some residents advertise rooms to let. Some of the restaurants in the village are also worth stopping for. Beyond Mogán a track leads to several inland lakes. This mountain landscape is a paradise for walkers, although the noise of four-wheel drive vehicles does tend to shatter the idyll.

Ideal country for a four-wheel drive

Barranco de Mogán

The peace of Veneguera is under threat

The C810, which from this point becomes progressively more adventurous (despite what some maps would have you believe), turns first towards the southwest, before continuing in a northerly direction again. After some 5km (3 miles) a signposted road leads off down the Barranco de Veneguera which ends at ★★ **Veneguera** and the sea. Visitors in search of empty beaches on Gran Canaria can find what they are looking for here and in the neighbouring bays. Veneguera is still lonely and tranquil, its fine dark sand inviting bathers. The neighbouring beaches at the end of the Barrancos of Tasarte and Tasartico, by contrast, are steep and stony. But the end of the idyll may not be far away. For some years a battle has raged in the courts and in the press regarding this beach. It was probably not an accident that the Playa de Veneguera, although in the centre of a conservation area, was released for building. It had been purchased by the Banesto Bank, the largest credit institute in Spain, which plans to construct a vast tourist complex here. It was projected that 40,000 hotel beds would be created, and there was even talk of a new airport. The bay was to be transformed into a new kind of holiday centre catering to luxury travellers. The scheme allows for detached villas set in parkland, in other words an average of 100sq m for each new bed, and no fewer than 6,000 newly planted trees.

However, all is not lost. The island's environmental lobbyists belonging to ASCAN have protested vehemently. The largest environmental and nature protection agency in Spain has its headquarters on Gran Canaria, and it has succeeded in stopping the scheme. Its aim is to preserve Veneguera from development. The outcome of the battle has not yet been decided: although planning permission was granted in 1992 the building works were postponed. There is, however, an almost-completed new road crossing the steep dividing watershed and linking Puerto de Mogán with the as yet still empty and beautiful Playa de Veneguera...

Barranco view
Papayas add some colour

Visitors with a four-wheel drive at their disposal will have no difficulty descending some of the other *barrancos* leading down to this stretch of coast. Each of them a miniature paradise, the gorges are contained by steep rock faces, and the valley floors are covered with waist-high reeds and palm trees. There are also little plantations of bananas, papayas and citrus fruits. After skidding along the gravel for some way you will eventually reach the sea and the island's last empty beaches.

The countryside was rather less idyllic for those who were once forced to make a living from the harvest provided by the narrow strip of land along the gorge floors. There are numerous abandoned farmhouses and terraces lying fallow. In 1950, the Barranco de Veneguera housed 700 registered inhabitants. Fewer than 100 are left today, and these are almost all older residents.

Returning to the C810, which winds its way through countless sharp bends past coloured rock walls (the tracks to the beaches of Tasarte and Tasartico lead off to the left), the route continues to **San Nicolás de Tolentino**, which since 1991 has officially been known as 'La Aldea de San Nicolás'. The local population refuses to accept the new name allotted to this agricultural centre of the west. Above the town the steep mountain walls recede to make way for a broad valley. The main crops grown here are tomatoes and cucumbers, as adequate water supplies are available from the huge storage reservoirs to the east of the village. Until a few years ago, the aromatic Canary Islands tomatoes were able to hold their own against their Dutch competitors. Recently, however, the market has also been contested by Morocco, which can supply the European Union with early vegetables at lower prices.

San Nicolás also suffers from the migration of its inhabitants. Since the mid-1980s, more than 20 percent of the almost 7,000 residents of this fertile valley have left their homes. Since the ambitious local tourist-development plans have not been realised either (a project to develop the beaches of Tasarte and Tasartico had to be abandoned after the entire coastline in the region was placed under a protection order), they see no future in this remote community.

The **Playa de San Nicolás** (or Playa de la Aldea) is stony and neglected. Apart from a number of little restaurants and bars frequented by the local inhabitants, it also offers the chance in the evening to watch the sun set behind the silhouette of Mount Teide on Tenerife.

A local visitor

Playa de la Aldea

61

One way of seeing the coast

A detour to the interior of the island is recommended to visitors with adequate experience of travelling across remote mountain tracks. You should turn off into the Barranco de la Aldea near San Nicolás de Tolentino. Passing a number of reservoirs, you will join Route 6 to the west of Artenara (*see page 68*). The trip is arduous but rewarding as it provides a glimpse of the island's variety of vegetation zones.

Worth seeing in any case is the rocky coastline stretching away to the north of the village. The cliffs plunge several hundred metres almost vertically down to the sea, scaled only by a serpentine road. Past Agaete, the road has been widened on four of the hairpin bends to create observation points. The ★★ **Mirador de Balcón** is particularly impressive and should be included in any tour of the western part of the island. On a clear day you can make out the Pico de Teide on Tenerife (3,718m/ 11,898ft), which is the highest mountain not only in the Canary Islands but also in the whole of Spain.

62

Cautious drivers will probably decide to return by the same route in order to get a better view of some of the scenic highlights which they flashed past on the outward journey. The more adventurous, however, may wish to continue along the road across the 'Green Mountains', as the rocky coast is exuberantly called. Constructed during the 1960s, it is well made but the northwards section crosses deep gorges and remains a hair-raising, if panoramic, experience.

El Risco is the only village of any size between here and Agaete (*see page 40*). If you prefer not to return by the same route, the only alternative is a time-consuming circuit of the entire island.

Mirador de Balcón

Route 6

The centre: tempest of Stone

Playa del Inglés – Roque Nublo – Artenara – Santa Lucía and back (200km/125 miles) *See map on page 64*

The Spanish writer and philosopher Miguel de Unamuno called the centre of the island 'Tempest of Stone'. The rocks shimmer in shades of red, yellow, gold and blue: precipices, monoliths rising heavenwards like giant fingers, jagged peaks, cliffs and cones. Over millions of years volcanic eruptions, wind and rain have moulded the country into every bizarre form imaginable. It is a wild, majestic setting which impresses every visitor. In this landscape lie gleaming white villages, clinging to the rock like Tejeda, or carved out of it like Artenara. From the roof of the island the view extends out across the sea to Tenerife, where the Pico de Teide, snow-capped in winter, hovers in the mist. Unless you have marvelled at this panorama you cannot claim to have seen Gran Canaria.

Visitors cling to their camels
Tejeda clings to the hillside

63

The formation of the island took place over a long period of time. The oldest rock samples have been estimated to be 16 million years old, whilst the youngest are only 500,000 years. In contrast to its neighbour La Palma, the volcanoes of Gran Canaria are considered to be extinct.

The highest peaks on the island lie in the centre. The Pico de las Nieves ('Peak of Snows') is the highest of all at 1,949m (6,395ft), followed by the Roque Nublo, the 'Rock of Clouds', at 1,803m (5,915ft). Deep *barrancos* radiate out from this central point, descending to sea level at the coast. Five main gorges branch out into 26 smaller canyons. These old lava channels have always served as the island's main arteries. Their fertile soil nurtures tropical and subtropical fruits, on their slopes grow the elegant pine trees and at the very top perch the undemanding almond trees whose blossoms clothe the rugged landscape in a cloud of pink in January and February. Apart from almonds, figs and citrus fruits are harvested and potatoes and other vegetables grown. Cattle are also kept, and it is quite possible that your way may suddenly be blocked by a herd of sheep or goats.

Before the Spanish conquered the island some five hundred years ago, the mountain peaks rose above dense pine forests. Centuries of indiscriminate felling have destroyed not only the trees but also the streams and rivers which once made Gran Canaria so fertile. If you go for a walk near Santa Lucía or Fataga you will have a glimpse of how green and lovely the island once was. At least the *pinar*, the pine forest, has been brought back to life by a

64

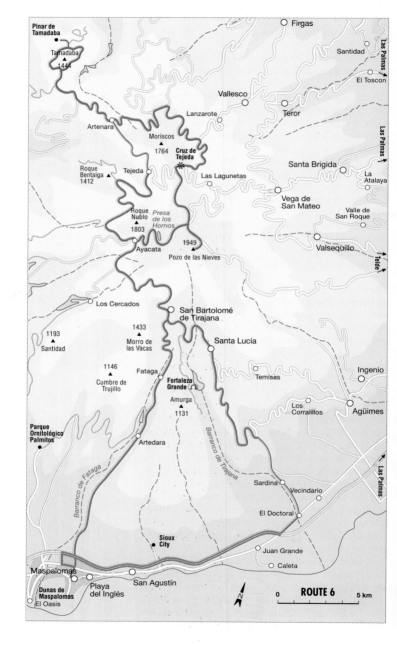

reforestation project near Tamadaba. Lichens, which hang from the trees like beards, show that the forest's worst enemy of our industrial times, air pollution, has not yet penetrated as far as this. The pine trees have a good chance of survival.

Nonetheless, the creation of this single area of green is not sufficient to restore the water supplies to their original level. Countless reservoirs (*embalses*) have been constructed to store the small amounts of water available from streams and rivers. This water is used to irrigate the fields and plantations, for which local well water is much too precious and expensive.

Visitors crossing the island from the south should leave the motorway near Playa del Inglés in the direction of Fataga (starting out from Las Palmas, the route can be followed in the opposite direction). After a short while, golden-coloured walls of rock with broad, pillar-like bands of basalt seem to crowd in on the **Barranco de Fataga**, somewhat reminiscent of the canyons featured in American western films.

A welcome watering hole

As the altitude increases, the valley becomes greener. Plantations of tropical fruits are spread out across the valley floor, and palm trees with feathery crowns grow along the roadside. Hovering above a precipice appears ★ **Fataga**, built on a rock jutting out into the gorge. The little village can offer neither historical sights nor a museum, but its pretty little alleys afford constantly changing, breathtaking views.

San Bartolomé de Tirjana

The road winds through countless bends towards the centre of the island. The signpost 'Mirador' to the right leads to a hotel whose terrace provides a magnificent view across the *barranco* as far as Santa Lucía. **San Bartolomé de Tirjana** is a historic, pretty little town. Founded in the 16th century, until recently it was the administrative centre of a region which included the tourist developments of Maspalomas and Playa del Inglés; today, its one claim to fame is the bustling market held every Sunday in front of the church.

San Bartolomé's principal source of income is fruit-growing. The fruit is used in the production of brandies, including 'Guindilla', a cherry liqueur. If you have time, take a stroll as far as the town hall, which boasts a flower-filled inner courtyard with a small gallery.

From San Bartolomé, follow the signs to Tejeda in order to reach the very centre of the 'Tempest of Stone'. Leaving the main road at the little village of Ayacata, follow the sign to 'Bentaiga/Cueva del Rey'. The first section of the track is asphalted but it soon degenerates to a gravel surface. The detour, however, is worthwhile.

Roque Bentaiga

Shade on the road to Cruz de Tejeda

★★ **Roque Bentaiga** is one of the most spectacular rock monoliths in the entire range, and the journey affords a succession of dramatic panoramas. At the foot of the Roque Bentaiga lies the last historically documented refuge of the original islanders, a complex of caves near the hamlet of **Roque**. The village itself unfortunately does not boast a bar, thus depriving the visitor of the chance of admiring the view over a cup of coffee. Nonetheless, a stroll through the village is rewarding. Behind the Roque some of the caves are still used as cattle sheds. There is also a fine view into the next *barranco*, including the villages of El Chorillo and El Espinillo. Not far away, but reachable only after an exhausting climb along a rocky path at the end of the track, lies the main cave complex. The largest of these is known as the **Cueva del Rey**, the 'King's Cave'. As there is little to see, however, the effort of getting there is hardly worthwhile.

The ★★ **Roque Nublo** has long been visible from the route. To reach this landmark of Gran Canaria, however, you must drive back onto the main road, thus retracing your route for a short distance before turning left at Ayacata. The 'Rock of Cloud' rises tall and narrow like a pointing finger; at 1,803m (5,915ft) it is the second-highest peak on the island. Depending on the time of day it shimmers gold or pale lilac, and viewed from the side it resembles a human face. The best view of the Roque Nublo can be had from a little parking bay on the left-hand side of the road. A narrow footpath leads to the top, and the hike, which takes about 30 minutes, is well worth the effort. Arriving on the rocky plateau you can gaze westwards towards the two monoliths known as 'Father' and 'Son', and you will understand why the first inhabitants of the island revered these rocks as a holy place.

Visitors who manage to get here early enough are usually rewarded with a clear view across the entire island. Over to the west is neighbouring Tenerife; to the north, at the foot of the mountain, you can see La Culata with Tejeda in the distance. In former times, incidentally, the 'Camino Real', one of the island's ancient trading routes, led from La Culata across the Roque Nublo and down to Ayacata. The path was just wide enough to enable two mules, laden with panniers on each side, to pass each other. Since the asphalt road was built at the foot of the mountain the old track has lost its significance; nonetheless, mountain-loving islanders have recently re-signposted and repaired it.

On the way back you will notice a rock rising bizarrely out of the ridge on the eastern side. With a little imagination it could be interpreted as having the form of a praying monk, which explains the name 'El Fraile'.

View from Cruz de Tejeda

Passing the dam Presa de los Hornos, the route continues towards Cruz de Tejeda past a sadly neglected picnic place which ironically bears the name 'La Huerta' after the nearby fruit orchards. About 3km (2 miles) after the reservoir, a road on the right leads to **Pico de las Nieves** (1,949m/6,395ft), the highest peak on the island, crowned by a radar station and TV transmitter. Pico de las Nieves means 'Peak of the Snows', but there is another name, Pozo de las Nueves, which relates to the local tradition of a well which became filled with compressed snow in the winter. Apparently, the ice remained frozen until summer and could then be transported to Las Palmas to be used for cooling patients during operations. The road passes around a military prohibited area and thence to an observation point from which there is a superb view of the Roque Nublo (*see page 66*). A second viewing point a little further on provides more splendid views of the surrounding hills, often as far as Teide on Tenerife – assuming, of course, that Pico de las Nieves is not shrouded in the dense clouds brought in by the trade winds.

67

The main roads in the centre of the island meet at the ★ **Cruz de Tejeda**, named after the stone crucifix which marks the top of the 1,520-m (4,987-ft) mountain pass. This is one of the regular stops on coach tours of the island, and there is a bustle of commercial activity, with stands selling fruit and sweets, donkey rides, etc. A few yards away, in an altogether more tranquil setting, is a state-run hotel, a *parador*, built in the 1930s in typical Canaries style to plans by Néstor de la Torre (*see page 27*). But business here doesn't seem to have been very brisk as for some years now only the restaurant has been in operation. There is a fine view from the terrace.

All roads meet at the cross

The road, which continues in the direction of Artenara, lives up to its reputation as both one of the most

The cave restaurant in Artenara

Pinar de Tamadaba

The church in Tejeda

beautiful, but also one of the most dangerous, stretches on the island. Visitors suffering from vertigo should refrain from looking over the edge at the steepest places.

★★ **Artenara**, at an altitude of 1,270m (4,167ft), is the highest village on Gran Canaria. It can also boast a further attraction: almost all the houses in the village and the surrounding hamlets are built into the solid rock. In Artenara there is even a **cave church**, recognised by the bell above the entrance. Some of the cave houses in the village are not immediately recognisable as such as they have normal, painted facades attached to their fronts. The inhabitants are not without modern amenites. However, what it must be like to live in such a house can be imagined after a visit to the **cave restaurant**. The establishment lies below the village centre where house No 9 marks the position of the long entrance tunnel. From the terrace in front there is a magnificent view of the Roque Bentaiga and Roque Nublo.

From Artenara it is worthwhile making a detour to the ★★ **Pinar de Tamadaba**, the only forest in the central massif and the finest on Gran Canaria. Large sections have been replanted with Canary pines. Blackened tree trunks reveal that forest fires are a perpetual problem; the Canary pine, however, seems to cope much better than other species. Many of the tall, slender trees have long lichens hanging from them.

Returning along the same road and driving back through Artenara, the route leaves the main road to follow a narrow minor road to **Tejeda**. The village enjoys a picturesque location at an altitude of 1,050m (3,444ft); its population numbers 980. Cracks are appearing in the idyll, however; terraced farming is no longer viable, and most inhabitants now commute to work in one of the main centres. The little church in the village centre is the only attraction for visitors. There are other reasons, however, behind the decline in agriculture. There are five reservoirs

within the community boundaries (Los Hornos, Soria, Parlillo, Cueva de las Niñas and Caidero de la Niña), but the water they contain does not belong to the village. Instead it is piped to Las Palmas, with the result that there is very little drinking water in Tejeda during the dry summer months.

Return now to San Bartolomé de Tirajana, but instead of continuing straight down the Barranco de Fataga, turn left just after the village along the C815 towards ★ **Santa Lucía**. This pretty village nestles between flower gardens and palm trees in the upper region of the **Barranco de Tirajana**, in one of the most romantic regions on the entire island. The feathery crowns of the palm trees form an attractive contrast to the stark rocks of the surroundings. The whitewashed houses of the village are clustered around the prominent domed church, which has a distinctly mosque-like appearance.

Santa Lucía

A restaurant with a difference

69

Don't miss the opportunity of stopping at **Hao**, one of the most popular local restaurants. It is not only worth a visit for the typical local speciality of roast kid from the grill, but also for its small **archaeological museum** run by the owner. Designed like a medieval castle, it houses his 'finds' including bones, Guanche mummies, tools, pottery and clothing from the pre-Spanish period. One of the special treasures of the private collection is a Roman amphora, dating from the 3rd century AD and found on the sea bed off Lanzarote. Don't be put off by the fact that the restaurant is often crowded; it is even worth stopping just for a beer under the pergola. Afterwards you can try the locally distilled liqueur 'Mejunje', a mixture of rum, honey and lemon.

Some 3km (2 miles) south of Santa Lucía, on the west side of the C815, is the **Fortaleza Grande**, a rock formation in the shape of a castle. Historical documents relate that it was one of the last refuges of the Guanches. From the road you can make out numerous caves and rock paths; there is a footpath, but it is advisable only to explore the area if you have appropriate equipment. The minimum requirements are stout shoes and a torch.

To the Guanches this was a sacred spot, and in April 1483, during the last days of the Spanish conquest, some 1,600 men, women and children entrenched themselves here until persuaded to surrender by their former chief, Tenesor Semidan (*see page 16*), who had been forcibly converted to Christianity. The event is still commemorated every year on 29 April.

The road descends through countless bends to the plain on the eastern side of the island, from where the motorway leads back to the starting point of the route.

CASA DE
COLON

Art History

Opposite: Casa Colón

Culture: Art History

Little remains today of the original art and culture of the Canary Islands. The first settlers left their pottery skills and farming techniques, whilst the conquerors brought Flemish paintings and the work of Moorish stonemasons and Andalusian carpenters. Folk music which originated in South America bears witness to the influence of returning emigrants on their homeland.

Ancient designs

Gran Canaria is dotted with evidence of pre-Spanish culture. There are elaborate systems of cave dwellings such as those at Cenobio de Valerón, as well as a number of cult sites such as the one at Montaña de las Cuatro Puertas (*see page 47*). Apart from pottery, rock drawings are all that remain of the early settlers' art. They have been found on the island in the form of geometric, sometimes coloured patterns, such as those of the Cueva Pintada (*see page 39*) The petroglyphs, known as *grabados*, were often decorated with coloured *pintadores* or stamps.

During excursions and walks through the island interior you will repeatedly come across natural stone houses, built without the use of mortar. Two concave walls of erratics are built facing each other, and the spaces in between the stones are filled in with detritus. Since winter frosts are unknown in Gran Canaria, such walls can last for centuries. It is thus possible the original islanders built their homes in this manner, and that the style of construction has been preserved until the present day.

Stone carving and the caves of Cenobio de Valerón

71

Architecture

The master builders responsible for many of the magnificent 16th-century buildings still standing today came from Andalusia. Even the lay observer will recognise this from the enclosed, ornately carved Moorish balconies, behind which the wives of prosperous citizens hid from the view of passers-by. The noblemen's houses in Gran Canaria have balconies with balustrades which are only waist-high, whereas those on the western islands were completely enclosed.

A typical balcony

The Moors were also the creators of the Mudéjar style. Those remaining in Spain after the Arabs had been expelled from the country converted to Catholicism but continued to decorate their buildings with geometrically-based designs. On the Canary Islands many churches and palaces boast wooden roofs built in the Mudéjar style. For religious reasons, Arab artists were forbidden to include representations of living creatures in their ornamentation. They thus sought inspiration in imaginative forms for which plants and geometric patterns formed the basis.

Churches contain a variety of treasures

On doorways and window supports you will often find Mudéjar elements, which were easily carved in the soft lava stone.

Churches and palaces which are at least 300 years old contain numerous paintings and altars by 16th- and 17th-century Flemish masters. This art reached the Canary Islands because at the time, the Netherlands was larger than today and formed part of the Spanish empire. The local merchants, having risen to prosperity as a result of the sugar trade, could afford to invite the leading artists of the time to work for them on Gran Canaria.

Painting

Geographical remoteness and the centuries of poverty of its inhabitants explain why the Canary Islands culture can boast little by way of indigenous creativity. César Manrique (1920–92), an artist who lived on Lanzarote and who was killed in an accident, is the only local artist to achieve world fame. His international reputation rests not only on his paintings and sculptures, but above all on his engagement as a nature conservationist. He fought to preserve the countryside from thoughtless building schemes. Néstor Martín Fernández de la Torre (1887–1938), Gran Canaria's most famous painter, was born in Las Palmas. His native town has dedicated a museum to him in the Pueblo Canario in Las Palmas (*see page 27*).

From Néstor's Poema de la Tierra

Literature

Pérez Galdós (1843–1920) has also achieved fame, at least on paper. His portrait adorns one side of the Ptas 1,000 banknote. Born in Las Palmas (*see page 25*) and known as the 'Iberian Balzac', his works are much read in Spain. Although he achieved fame for his historical novels and dramas, Galdós only attained national recognition after he had moved his place of residence to Madrid and Toledo.

Pérez Galdós

Handicrafts

The legacy of the original inhabitants of the islands, collectively known as the Guanches (*see page 17*) can clearly be seen in the local pottery. Terracotta stamps (Spanish = *pintaderas*) were used in order to print patterns on cloth. The art of ceramics was traditionally practised by the women and reveals definite similarities with the pottery of North Africa. This is one of the pieces of evidence pointing to a link between the North African Berbers and the Guanches. The pots were formed without a potter's wheel and thus have no 'foot'. They were made by placing strips of black clay on top of each other and are decorated with fine, mostly naive motifs. On Gran Canaria colours are also used. Today such pots make valued, if slightly expensive, gifts or souvenirs.

Festivals and Folklore

Music

Emigrants returning from South America brought with them more modern elements. No fiesta today would be complete without *salsa* rhythms, which can be clearly distinguished from the basic rhythms of the native folk music and dances of the Canary Islands. The local songs reveal primarily the influence of Andalusian and North African music.

Fiestas

On Gran Canaria, as in other Spanish speaking countries throughout the world, each town and village celebrates an annual fiesta, mostly to mark the festival of the patron saint. Such fiestas usually last for two weekends and the intervening week. The events always include folkloric performances, food, drink and dancing (not before 10pm).

Thanks to the summer-like temperatures, the Pre-Lenten Carnival on Gran Canaria is also the occasion for colourful celebrations in the streets. South American customs are mixed with Catholic ritual. Brightly-coloured masked figures throng the streets to wild samba sounds in the wake of the Carnival Queen, elected the day before and accompanied by ceremonial gunfire. Incidentally, the Canary Island revellers seldom stick religiously to the official carnival calendar: the party is hardly ever over by Ash Wednesday, and even later there will be gatherings at which uniformed choirs organised by the carnival committees make fun of local politics. Traditionally, the carnival ends with the 'Burial of the Sardine', another custom which originated in South America. To the sounds of riotous merrymaking, an enormous papier-mâché sardine is carried in funeral procession.

High spirits in Agaete

Festive symbol

Festival Calendar

There are also a large number of major festivals celebrated by the entire island population:

January 6: Feast of the Epiphany. On this day, children in Spain receive their Christmas presents instead of Christmas Day. In Las Palmas and other larger towns, the Three Kings (*Los Reyes*), ride into the town throwing sweets for the children.

February Almond-Blossom Festival in Tejeda and Valsequillo. The exact date depends on the timing of the blossom and is laid down by the local council. Traditional handicrafts, dancing and sports displays all form a part of the festivities.

February/March The Carnival celebrations on Gran Canaria bear more resemblance to Rio than Venice. Revellers in brightly coloured costumes dance all night on the streets and squares. The celebrations are particularly riotous in Las Palmas and Playa del Inglés.

June Corpus Christi. The streets of the Old Town and the Plaza Santa Ana in Las Palmas, as well as the town square in Arucas, are carpeted with decorative patterns of flowers or coloured sand or salt.

Bajada de la Rama is on August 4

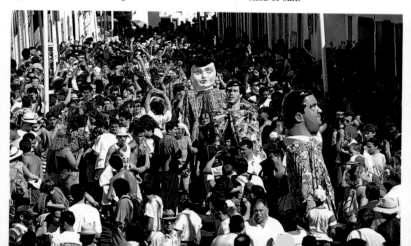

24: Feast of St John (San Juan). Bon-fires are lit on many hilltops, and there are major celebrations in Telde, Las Palmas and Arucas.

July   16: Feast of St Carmen, patron saint of fishermen. Festivals with boat processions are held in all ports.

August   4: Bajada de la Rama, the 'Procession with the Branches', is held in Agaete and the neighbouring port of Puerto de la Nieves. The festival is pagan in origin and symbolises prayers for fertility and rain. The villagers carry branches from the mountains to the sea and whip the waves.

September   8: Island Festival celebrating the feast of the patron saint of Gran Canaria, the Virgen del Pino. The faithful and a large crowd of onlookers gather for the procession in Teror.
10: Around this date the inhabitants of San Nicolás de Tolentino celebrate the Fiesta der Charco, the 'Festival of the Puddle'. The climax is reached when the participants throw each other into the water.

October   6: Festival of the Sea in the ports of Las Palmas and Santa Brigida.

Lucha Canaria

Canary Islands wrestling was probably a sport practised by the original inhabitants of the islands. In almost every place there is a sandy ring on which contests are held. There are two teams of twelve wrestlers, who take it in turns to face a member of the opposing team. The aim is to throw the opponent to the floor, and all parts of the body may be used except the feet. The short trousers with rolled-up legs worn by the contestants provide a grip. After a maximum of three rounds the winner is the team which has lost the fewest wrestlers. *Lucha Canaria* is the most popular traditional sport on the islands and can be seen at every local fiesta. Competitions also take place in Las Palmas in the Estadio López Socas.

Juego de palo is like singlesticks, except two sticks are used by each contestant instead of one. The object is to move the body as little as possible while attacking and fending off the blows of an opponent.

Wrestling bout in progress

75

Food and Drink

Gran Canaria can offer culinary delights to satisfy every taste: from gourmet temples to simple country inns, you will find good, not necessarily inexpensive, restaurants on every corner. Of course there are establishments – mostly in the south – where the tourist will find such familiar delights as fish and chips and spaghetti bolognese. Tracking down a little fishermen's pub or a *parilla* outside the main tourist centres with typical local specialities and 'vino del pais', the local Canary wine, is more difficult. Such restaurants seldom boast a menu, although there may be a slate listing the dishes available that day (remember to pack a dictionary!).

Where to eat

Where can you buy what? The *kiosco* sells not newspapers but coffee, refreshments and perhaps at most a *bocadillo*, a sandwich. Coffee, incidentally, is available on the Canary Islands in three variations which are drunk at any time of day: *café solo* (black), *cortado* (with a little milk or cream) and *café con leche* (coffee with milk). A *kiosco* will be found on almost every square in even the smallest village and serves as a popular meeting place for a gossip amongst the locals at any time of day, morning, noon and night.

The same applies to the bar, which has nothing to do with nightlife, but is a type of local pub. They will be found on every village street and in all districts of a town. Closing time is usually 11pm. Almost all drinks are available, but the only food available is *tapas* – small snacks which can be chosen from a display in a glass case. *Tapa* is the Spanish word for 'lid', and the name derives from the custom of placing a small plate on top of the wine glass to keep out flies. Bar-keepers soon had the idea of putting a small appetiser on the plate, and the tradition of *tapas* was born.

A *parilla* ('grill') is a rustic inn with wooden tables and benches and rough wooden walls. The menu consists of grilled meat and occasionally fish. The best example of a *parilla* is the Hao in Santa Lucía (*see page 69*). The food is quite simple and the prices modest. Outside the main tourist centres, a *restaurante* is usually a relatively unpretentious inn.

Specialities

Don't miss the local specialities such as fresh fish, which is certain to have been landed at the nearest port that very morning. The locals prefer *merluza*, *vieja* or *bonito* – hake, parrot fish and a kind of tuna. But in fact a true fishermen's tavern will serve seafood in unimaginable variety, although

Opposite: Snacking at Sardina

The kiosco in Parque San Telmo

A good choice of fish

not every species is available all the year round. In season you will find *langostinos* and mackerel, moray, sardines and limpets.

The fish is served with *papas arrugadas*, 'wrinkled' potatoes. The method stems from the fishermen who used to boil the well-scrubbed, unpeeled potatoes in salted water (or, even better, in seawater) until the water has evaporated and formed a salt crust round the wrinkled potatoes. The skin with its salt crust are also eaten. Fish and potatoes are usually accompanied by *mojo verde*, a green sauce; meat is served with *mojo rojo*, a spicier, reddish version prepared with garlic, chilli, vinegar and olive oil.

Meat dishes are often available as *carne de cerdo* or *chuleta* – grilled pork escalope or chop. Also popular are *cabrita*, kid, and *conejo*, rabbit, which may be served *en salsa* (with sauce).

Other specialities include a range of filling soups and stews: *garbanza* (chick-pea soup) or *sopa picadilla* (vegetable soup with egg), as well as *puchero*, the most famous of the traditional stews. In a typical *parilla* they will all be served with *gofio*, the Canary Islands' most famous speciality.

Made of wheat, barley or a mixture of the two, *gofio* was the staple food of the original inhabitants of the Canary Islands. If no cereals were available it was made of the roots of ferns. When the islands were colonised the conquerors took over this wholefood dish, and it still forms an essential part of the local diet today. To prepare *gofio*, wholemeal flour is roasted before being ground. The roasting process replaces more orthodox baking or cooking methods, and the *gofio* is then ready to be eaten. Further cooking turns the *gofio* into 'cemento'. Islanders take *gofio* with them when they go hunting or to work in the fields; kneaded to 'sausages' with water, it makes a complete meal. For children it is stirred into milk, whilst the entire family will sprinkle it onto soups. Sauces are thickened with gofio, and even wine tastes good mixed with the slightly malty taste. Local inhabitants claim that eating *gofio* three times a day accounts for their remarkable physical strength.

Favourite desserts include the delcious *bienmesabe*, a highly calorific sweet dish prepared from almonds and honey, or *queso blanco*, the piquant goat's cheese. Particularly recommended on Gran Canaria is *queso de flor*, a sweetish cheese made of cow's and sheep's milk with the addition of thistle leaves.

In addition to the strongly flavoured, sometimes rather heavy local wines (eg Malvasía), all of which are produced on neighbouring islands, the Canary Islands are also famous for a light beer which is produced locally under the brand names 'Dorada' and 'Tropical'.

Promenade restaurant

A selection of local wines

Restaurant selection

The following are suggestions for just a few of the more popular spots on the island. They are listed according to the following categories: $$$ = expensive; $$ = moderate; $ = cheap

Eating out in Puerto de Mogán

Las Palmas

$$$**Hamburgo**, General Orgaz 54, tel: 222745. The German gourmet establishment has more to offer than just *sauerkraut* and dumplings – albeit at a price (closed Wednesday and Sunday). $$**El Padrino**, Jesús Nazareno 1, tel: 462094. This fish restaurant on La Isleta is not only famous for its Canary Islands seafood specialities. On warm summer evenings you can sit here outside and revel in the marvellous view and the peace and quiet (closed Thursday; can be reached by Bus No 42 from Santa Catalina Park). $$**El Herreño**, Medizábal 5, tel: 310513. The 'Man from El Hierro' near the Old Town market serves simple food from the smallest island in the archipelago: wine, cheese and sometimes *gofio*. $$**The Balalaika**, Fernando Guanarteme 27, tel: 274483. Caviar is affordable in this Russian restaurant, and everything else is worth trying (closed Sunday). $$**China House Ming**, Luis Morote 36, tel: 274563. Visitors who can't do without spring rolls and classical Chinese cuisine even on holiday will find the menu at Ming's near the Playa de las Canteras just right.

Do not forget the restaurants in the better hotels, where you can eat without being a guest of the hotel. Treat yourself, for example, to a meal or even just a coffee in the **Reina Isabel** ($$$) on the beachfront promenade, or a meal with a view in the tower of **Los Bardinos** ($$$).

Mogán

$$$**Acayama**, Tostador 14, tel: 569263, is considered one of the best on the island – and not just because of the view.

Playa del Inglés

$$**La Estancia** (in the 'Cita' shopping centre), tel: 762787. Spanish cuisine à la carte. $$**Las Cumbres**, Avenida de Tirajana 9, tel: 760941. Speciality: lamb, Spanish-style.

Puerto de Mogán

$$**El Barranco**, Rivera del Carmen 2, tel: 565542. The international specialities are very good and not too expensive (closed Monday). $$**Tono's Restaurant**, by the harbour, tel: 565186. Don't miss the fresh fish.

Santa Lucía

Hao, tel: 798007. Typical *parilla* serving fresh kid from the grill. Also a museum and an enchanting pergola.

Hao also has a museum

Nightlife

Las Palmas

As everywhere in Southern Europe, much of the nightlife in Las Palmas takes place on the streets. Canary Islanders need no clubs to find entertainment at night. Spontaneous chats in the park, dance music spilling out onto the pavements and convivial drinking on the beach are commonplace, and holidaymakers wishing to join in the fun are often welcome.

This means that nightclubs and discos are primarily for foreign visitors, although in recent years Saturday Night Fever seems to have infected the young people of Las Palmas too. In most discotheques, very little happens before midnight, e.g. **Zorba's**, Luis Morote, **Toca Toca**, Plaza de España, **Jet**, Avenida Bethencourt and **Utopia**, Tomás Miller. In addition, most of the larger hotels have a disco, dance bar or nightclub which are also open to non-hotel residents. At present, the favourite 'in' nightspots are **Dinos** in Los Bardinos Hotel in Santa Catalina and **El Coto** in the Hotel Cristina.

Playa del Inglés

There are also large numbers of discothèques and night clubs in the tourist centres on Gran Canaria, particularly in Playa del Inglés. Near the 'Kasbah' **Pacha** is elegant and expensive and therefore popular with the local *papagallos*; **Joy** and **Garage** are for disco professionals. There are flamenco shows in the **Aladinos** night club.

Casinos

Propping up the bar in Las Palmas

There are two casinos on the island, one in the Hotel Tamarindos in San Agustín and the other in the Hotel Santa Catalina in Las Palmas.

Active Holidays

Walking

Gran Canaria offers plenty of opportunities for walks to suit every interest and physical condition. You can wander for weeks unaccompanied through the dense vegetation of the *barrancos*, or follow a guide along wide, easy paths. For some time work has been in progress to repair, signpost and maintain the *caminos reales*, the former trading routes. A book listing these paths can be purchased in the bookshops of Las Palmas. Even easy day trips, however, require a certain amount of careful preparation. You should never set out on an excursion completely alone, nor should you rely completely on the map. Furthermore, it is advisable to wear ankle-high walking boots, to set off before lunch and to always carry sun protection cream and some waterproof clothing.

Guided walks are offered by a number of hotels and local travel agencies. One popular choice is 'Viajes Maspalomas', tel: 764195. Cheaper and less professional, but no less informative, are the walks organised by 'Grupo Montañero Mogán', tel: 561204, a walking association of local islanders and residents of all nationalities.

Golf in Maspalomas

Golf and riding

There are two **golf courses** on the island: Campo de Golf de Maspalomas, tel: 762581 and Campo de Bandama in Los Toscones, tel: 351050. Both course are 18-hole. The Bandama club also has a **riding** school, tel: 351290. Horses can also be hired at the Rancho Park (near Palmitos), which also organises pony treks into the mountains.

Watersports

Deep-sea fishing is a popular activity on the Canaries. The mecca of this sport on Gran Canaria is Puerto Rico, from where boats regularly depart on deep-sea expeditions. Further information can be obtained from 'Maritima Insular', Puerto Rico, tel: 745018. The coastal waters also offer ideal conditions for **diving and snorkelling**. Many hotels offer courses.

The marina at Puerto de Mogán

Gran Canaria also offers ideal conditions for **sailing and windsurfing**, although the strong winds on some stretches of coast make these areas unsuitable for beginners. The south and south-west coasts are the safest, and surfboards can be hired at all the main beach resorts. Sailing courses are offered at Puerto Rico.

Further activities

You can also go parachuting or paragliding (Aeroclub Tarajillo, tel: 247393), cycling (bicycle hire San Agustín, tel: 763829) or even join a camel safari (in Fataga).

Getting There

Gran Canaria can be reached by sea or by air. The average flight time from England is 4 hours; by ship, the voyage from the port of Cadiz on the Spanish mainland takes two and a half days.

By air

The Spanish national airline Iberia runs three flights a week from London to Las Palmas. It is also possible to fly from international airports around the world to Madrid and pick up a domestic flight there. There are also numerous charter flights to Las Palmas from London and other European cities. These are usually part of a package which includes accommodation.

Gran Canaria's international airport, the Aeropuerto de Gando, is situated 22km (14 miles) south of the capital, Las Palmas. There is no shuttle bus service from the airport. Visitors who are not met by a tour operator's representative will have to take the SALCAI bus which stops on the motorway near the airport on its way from the central bus station in Las Palmas to Playa del Inglés. The bus stop (ask for the *parada de la guagua*) is five minutes' walk from the airport. The trip from the airport into town by taxi costs approximately Ptas 3,000.

By sea

If you are travelling by ship you will reach Gran Canaria on the ferry run by the national steamship company Compañia Trásmediterranea. The voyage from Cadiz to Las Palmas takes 50 hours. Although the ferry has a pool and various restaurants on board, the trip is by no means a joy ride: there is no entertainment programme, and the sea is often rough.

A recommended alternative is a special service offered by Iberia during the summer months: your car sets off by sea and you fly two days later from Seville. Contact your travel agent for further details.

Inter-island ferry

Island-hopping

Iberia and its subsidiaries Aviaco and Binter Canarias operate several flights each day from Gando airport to all the other islands in the archipelago except La Gomera, which still has no airport. Inter-island ferries leave daily from the 'Puerto de la Luz' in Las Palmas for Tenerife (where you should change for La Palma, El Hierro and La Gomera), and three times per week for Lanzarote and Fuerteventura.

The car ferry to Tenerife takes four hours for the 63-km (39-mile) crossing. The jetfoil is quicker, taking only 80 minutes.

Getting Around

The only public transport

Bus

The only public transport vehicles on Gran Canaria are the buses (*guaguas*). There is a comprehensive network of routes crossing the island and linking the tourist centres. With a little advance planning, even excursions and walks can be organised by bus. For this it is necessary to acquire the latest version of the timetable issued half-yearly by the SALCAI bus company (south, west and east) and by UTINSA (north). It can be obtained at the central bus station in Las Palmas (Estación de Guaguas) at San Telmo Park, tel: 360179 (Monday to Friday 6am–10pm) and in Playa del Inglés, Shop No 442 in the Yumbo shopping centre (9am–1.30pm and 3.30–6pm).

You will have no difficulty using the bus route between Las Palmas and Maspalomas (buses run every 15 minutes), between Las Palmas and Puerto Rico (buses run every 30 minutes) and between San Agustín and Maspalomas. Along other routes the bus services are designed to serve the local population.

Within Las Palmas, a number of local buses run between Vegueta Old Town and the harbour. There are bus stops by the Teatro Pérez Galdós (Plaza de Stagno) and at the Plaza Cairasco.

Taxi

There is no shortage of taxis which can flagged down as they drive past. For journeys within town, the fare is calculated according to the meter. For longer journeys out of town the fare should be negotiated in advance.

By car

The easiest way of exploring the island or even making short trips is to rent a car. The roads are mostly of European standard, and traffic signs and rules of the road will also mostly be familiar. However, a few Spanish warning signs and regulations should be noted:

carretera cerrada = road blocked
ceda el paso = observe priority
desprendimentos = danger of avalanches
desvio = detour

Seat belts must be worn in Spain, as must crash helmets by motorbike riders. There are high penalties for illegal parking (apart from the familiar international signs, no-parking zones are indicated by yellow marks on the kerb), for speeding (the speed limit in built-up areas is 50kph (30mph), elsewhere 90kph (56mph) except on motorways and motorway-type roads (100kph/ 62mph) and for driving a vehicle with faults. It is advisable to examine the condition of a rented vehicle before signing the contract.

Keep to the speed limit

84

Many roads have spectacular views

On Gran Canaria there are a number of dubious rental agencies which try to attract customers with bargain offers. To avoid problems, however, it is advisable to settle for one of the larger, if possible international, rental firms, e.g. (airport) Hertz, tel: 579577; Avis, Tel: 579578; (Las Palmas) Hertz, tel: 226497; Avis, tel: 275567; OCCA, tel: 275440; (south coast) Cigar, tel: 761534. You should ask for any special reductions or bargain. A small car, e.g. Seat Panda, costs about the same as anywhere else in Europe; a four-wheel drive costs about twice as much. It is always advantageous to agree on a rental period of three days or a week. Do not be tempted to economise on the insurance – minor bumps are a commonplace event and even in such a trivial affair you will be at a disadvantage compared with a local driver. Many car rental firms also have *mopeds* for hire. Since just about every Canary Islander also has a 'moto', two-stroke mixture is easily available at garages.

Petrol on the Canary Islands is cheaper than just about anywhere else in Europe. Petrol stations (*gasolineras*) are mostly open until 10pm, although like other establishments many close during the siesta between 2–5pm.

If you rent a car on Gran Canaria you would do well to remember that the traffic police with their notorious breakdown truck ('*la grua*') sometimes appear within minutes to tow away illegally parked cars. This applies particularly in Las Palmas. Tracking down a car which has 'disappeared' in this manner can cost a stranger half a day's holiday and a lot of bother in addition to the hefty fine.

By bicycle

Bicycles and mountain bikes are popular with visitors and locals alike. Since charter airlines no longer transport sports vehicles free of charge, rental has become a viable proposition once more. New firms open every day.

First aid at Maspalomas

Facts for the Visitor

Travel documents

Visitors from European Union countries, the Commonwealth and the United States must have a valid passport. No visa is required by nationals of the EU, Australia, Canada or New Zealand for a stay of up to three months, or by US nationals for a stay of up to six months. Visitors bringing their own car will need the vehicle registration documents and a green insurance certificate. National driving licences are accepted in the case of visitors staying less than six months on the island.

Customs

There are now no limits to the amounts of goods imported from one European Union country to another, provided they are for personal use and have been purchased in an EU country. However, the customs authorities have issued a list of maximum amounts of alcholic drinks, tobacco goods, perfumes, etc. For those coming direct from a country outside the EU, the allowances for any such goods are: 200 cigarettes or 100 cigarillos or 50 cigars or 250g tobacco; 1 litre spirits or 2 litres fortified wine or 3 litres table wine; 60cc perfume; 250cc toilet water.

The status of free-trade zone that has benefited the islands so much in the past is under threat from the EU and is likely to be phased out by 1996.

Currency and exchange

Unlimited amounts of foreign currency can be brought into the country. If the sum exported exceeds Ptas 500,000 it must be declared. Spanish currency can be imported in unlimited amounts and exported in amounts of up to Ptas 1 million per person without declaration.

Tourist information

In the UK: Spanish Tourist Office, 57–58 St James's Street, London SW1A 1LD, tel: (0171) 499 0901.
In the US: Tourist Office of Spain, 665 Fifth Avenue, New York, NY 10022, tel: 212-759 8822, fax: 212-980 1053; 8383 Wilshire Blvd, Suite 960, Beverly Hills, Ca 90211, tel: 213-658 7188, fax: 213-658 1061.

On Gran Canaria

Information concerning the entire island can be obtained from the Patronato de Turismo, León y Castillo 17, Las Palmas, tel: 362422, fax: 362822 (Monday to Friday 9am–3pm, Saturday 9am–1pm).

Las Palmas
There are several tourist information offices in Las Palmas. The most important is located in the Parque Santa Catalina in the traditional Canary Islands house on the side facing the harbour, tel: 264623, fax: 229820 (Monday to Friday 9am–1.30pm and 5–7pm, Saturday mornings only). A second office in the Pueblo Canario, Parque Doramas, is only open during the folklore performances, tel: 243593.

Playa del Inglés
Centro Insular de Turismo, Avenida de España/Avenida de Norteamericana (near the Yumbo shopping centre), tel: 762585, fax: 762591 (weekdays 9am–9pm)

Puerto de Mogán
Lokal 329 (by the harbour), tel: 565428 (Monday to Friday 10am–2pm and 4–6pm)

Money

The national currency is the Spanish peseta (Pta), which has been subjected to considerable fluctuations in exchange rates following three devaluations during the past three years. One thing, however, is certain: holidays on the Canary Islands have become steadily less expensive during the past few years.

Coins are available in the following denominations: 1, 5, 10, 25, 100, 200 and 500 Ptas, and banknotes to the value of 1,000, 2,000, 5,000 and 10,000 Ptas. In remote places you will probably have to present your passport when cashing a Eurocheque (maximum amount: Ptas 25,000). In towns and holiday complexes credit cards and cash dispensers are widely used.

Tipping

In a restaurant or when travelling by taxi, you should round up the total sum as you would do at home. Approximately 10 percent is the usual amount.

Cash dispensers are everywhere

Opening Times

There are no official opening hours.

Shops are open Monday to Friday 9am–1pm and 5–7pm, supermarkets 5–8pm. On Saturdays most shops are only open in the morning, although shops in tourist centres are also open on Saturday afternoons and Sundays. From July to September, shops (except supermarkets) are usually open during the morning only, but close at 2pm instead of 1pm. Special regulations apply in tourist centres.

Banks are open Monday to Friday 8.30–2pm. They are also open on Saturdays except during the months of July–September.

Post Offices (*correos*) are open Monday to Friday 8am–2pm, on Saturday until 1pm.

Public Holidays

Spain has not only national but also regional and local public holidays. You might find all the shops in one village closed, whilst in the next town it is business as usual. The following holidays are observed on the island: 1 January (New Year), 6 January (Epiphany), 19 March (Festival of St Joseph), Good Friday, Easter Sunday, 1 May (May Day), Whit Sunday, Ascension Day, Corpus Christi, 30 May (Dia de Canarias, regional holiday), 25 July (Festival of St James), 15 August (Assumption), 12 October (Discovery of America), 1 November, 6 December (Constitution Day), 8 December (Immaculate Conception), 25 December (Christmas Day). If a holiday falls on a Sunday, it is postponed until the following Monday.

Shopping and souvenirs

The Canary Islands were scheduled to lose their status as a free trade (duty-free) zone by 1996, so the savings on items such as tobacco, spirits, perfume, cosmetics, watches, jewellery, electronic and optical equipment may no longer as great as they once were.

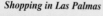

Shopping in Las Palmas

The shopping centres in the main tourist destinations, as well as department stores in the capital, are geared to holidaymakers and carry a wide range of goods. Bargaining is expected on the flea markets of Las Palmas and the streetside stands in Playa del Inglés, where trading is in the hands of North African merchants. You should never pay the first price quoted. The shops and stores along the Avenida de Mesa y López sell fine shoes and textiles; you will find electrical and electronic goods in the bazaars of Santa Catalina; souvenirs in the Old Town; fruit, vegetables and fish at all times in the covered market in the Calle Galicia, while the covered market by the harbour (Calle Lopez Sorcas) specialises in second-hand items. These, however, are better still on the **Rastro**, the flea market held on Sundays on the Avenida de Mesa y López or on the promenade behind the covered markets by the harbour.

A good place to hunt for typical local souvenirs (embroidery, basketware, pottery) is **Artesanía Canaria Tagügüy** in the Old Town of Las Palmas, near the Columbus House (Armas 1, Vegueta). Traditional Guanche pottery dishes and will be found, for example, at the shop run by Maria Hernandéz Alonso in the Calle Maestro in Santa Brígida. Made in the traditional manner by women without the assistance of a potter's wheel and then placed to dry in the sun, this type of pottery is not exactly cheap but is nonetheless unique. Embroidery is especially good value in Ingenio, e.g. in the Centro Artesanía beside the church. The motifs are taken directly from nature and feature a variety of designs; they often adorn traditional local costumes.

Embroiderer at work

The small knives used by banana workers (cuchillos canarios) will probably end up being used to open letters at home. They have a wide blade and a handle decorated with inlaid patterns and can be bought at **Roberto Moreno** in the Atalaya district of Guía.

The brightly patterned basketware goods made of palm fronds should not be confused with the straw baskets imported from Taiwan. Typical products will be found e.g. on the handicrafts market held on the first Sunday of every month on the Plaza de Santiago in Gáldar.

It is wise to resist the temptation to take culinary specialities home with you. *Mojo* and *bienmesabe* don't taste nearly as good in temperate climes. And you should also beware of 'special offers' from mostly African traders whose goods include ivory jewellery or leather or fur goods from endangered species. Not only will you be supporting the extermination of rare animals, but the import of such items into Europe and the US is forbidden and subject to heavy penalties.

Postal Services

All letters and postcards from the Canaries go by air. Mail takes at least five days to reach northern Europe. Postage stamps (*sellos*) can be purchased in post offices, tobacconists' shops (*tabacos*), at hotel reception desks and in souvenir shops selling postcards. Spanish post-boxes are a distinctive yellow.

Telephone

International calls can be made from coin-operated public telephones bearing the word *internacional*. These accept Ptas 25, 50, 100 or 500 coins or a telephone card (available for Ptas 1000 or Ptas 2000). To be recommended are the telephone shops (*locutorios*) in the larger towns or the *teléfonos públicos* in remote hamlets, as you can pay

You can't miss the telephones

the sum registered on the meter at the end of the conversation. More pleasant, if expensive, is to make your phone calls through the hotel exchange.

To make an overseas call, dial 07 and wait for the signal, then dial the international code (UK 44; US and Canada 1) followed by the local code (omitting the initial zero from numbers in the UK) and the subscriber's number. The code for the Canary Islands from overseas is 3428 (preceded by the relevant international access code). The cheap rate applies from 10pm–8am.

Time
As the Canary Islands use GMT there is no time difference to the United Kingdom. Summer Time (GMT + 1) also applies during the summer months.

Electricity
In tourist centres the voltage is 220v. Elsewhere 110v is the rule. Adapters may be necessary.

Clothing
Take with you the type of clothing you would wear at home during the summer months. Don't forget suntan lotion with a high protection factor and a sunhat. Bear in mind any particular requirements. If you plan to walk along the beach, you will need sandals because of the heat of the sand. For elegant restaurants a jacket or more formal dress will be appropriate as the Canary Islanders like to dress up for the occasion when they go out for dinner. A sweatshirt, anorak and walking boots will be useful for mountain walks as sudden changes in the weather are commonplace. If you visit Gran Canaria during the winter you will be glad of a pullover at night. Bare legs and shoulders are frowned upon in churches.

Photography
There's a vast assortment of photographic material and equipment available in the Canary Islands, and prices are around the same as those in Europe. Many of the tourist centres have overnight development services too.

Yesterday's news

Newspapers
In the tourist centres along the south coast, English newspapers are usually available on the day of issue. They appear one day later in Las Palmas and on the newspaper stand in the Parque Santa Catalina. Local news and events are listed in *Info Canarias*.

Medical assistance
It is advisable to take out insurance for private treatment in the case of an illness or accident. Nationals of non-EU

countries should certainly do this. With Form E111 from the Department of Health and Social Security, UK visitors are entitled to reciprocal medical treatment in Spain, but the document must be presented at the Spanish Social Insurance department in Las Palmas (Instituto Nacional de la Seguridad Social, León y Castillo 224, tel: 232299) in order to obtain a Spanish entitlement certificate. This must then be presented to an approved doctor. As a rule, it is much easier to see a doctor privately for treatment, to pay for his services and to claim reimbursement after returning home.

The same applies to bills for medicines. The *farmacias* on Gran Canaria, at least in the tourist centres, stock all medicines available elsewhere in Europe, often at a cheaper price. As the brand names are not always identical, however, it is advisable to seek one of the larger establishments where the different brand names under which medicines are known in other countries are listed by computer.

You are unlikely to encounter language problems when seeking a doctor or a chemist in the main tourist centres, since English is widely spoken. Hotels keep lists of English-speaking doctors in the vicinity.

Emergencies
There are emergency numbers common to all the islands: **091** (police) and **222222** (medical emergencies). In addition, there are specific numbers to call for Gran Canaria: **Police**, tel: 251100 (Las Palmas), 740000 (Mogán), 762898 (Maspalomas).
Medical Emergency Service (24 hours), tel: 259742 (Las Palmas), 763684 (Costa Canaria).

Crime
Crime is a contentious subject on Gran Canaria. Officials tend to play it down, while the press exaggerates it. You must be prepared for pickpockets in the Parque Santa Catalina and beach bandits in Maspalomas. Small change is most safely carried on your person, e.g. in a money belt. Valuables and documents should be placed in the hotel safe for safekeeping (there are also lockers on the larger beaches). Cars are an inviting target.

If the worst happens, a police report issued by the Guardia Civil will be required in order to substantiate an insurance claim.

Diplomatic Representation
United Kingdom: Edificio Cataluña, Calle de Luis Morote 6 (3rd floor), Las Palmas, tel: (928) 271259.
United States: Calle José Roca 5, Las Palmas, tel: (928) 271259.

Most hotels have pools

Accommodation

The hotel register for Gran Canaria lists hundreds of hotels, in all categories and price classes, and thousands of apartment blocks and bungalow complexes. Nonetheless, searching for accommodation on the spot can be an arduous business as most establishments will have been booked en bloc by tour operators from England and Germany. This means that the hoteliers themselves are not allowed to let even empty rooms if they are theoretically occupied. However, this rule applies only to the 'German Season', from Christmas until Easter, and also only to accommodation on the coast. Experience has shown that away from the beach you will always find something available, whatever your price range.

Visitors wishing to travel independently should not automatically assume that they will find somewhere to stay in every pretty little town in the interior or along the north coast. Teror, for example, which is the most important place of pilgrimage on the island, has not a single guest bed to offer visitors.

Hotels on Gran Canaria start in the five-star category. A separate bathroom, double bed and sitting area are standard. The four and five-star ratings correspond with international norms; a luxury-class room costs approximately Ptas 14,000, while a superior room costs about Ptas 10,000 including breakfast.

Paradores sign

Paradores are state-run hotels which are usually beautifully sited at places of particular interest. They offer every comfort and amenity and have well-trained staff.

Hostales are the equivalent of a pension or boarding house. In a two-star establishment you can expect a shower in your room; one-star accommodation will normally only have a shared shower along the corridor. Breakfast will be available in the bar across the road, and regular room service is not always provided. The price, however, is likely to be less than Ptas 2,500.

An **apartamento** is a holiday flat and should be just that. It should contain at least two rooms, plus bathroom and kitchen with cooking equipment. Apartamentos are awarded between one and three keys instead of stars. They are increasing in popularity and provide a relatively inexpensive and comfortable alternative to hotel accommodation, particularly for families with children. They also serve as a comfortable home-from-home for the large number of Europeans who own no property here, but who choose to spend the winter on Gran Canaria.

A **studio** is a one-room apartment without kitchen.

Bungalows are holiday homes and must have more than two rooms and be free-standing. They usually also have a small garden.

Fincas, or 'farmhouses', are holiday flats, studios or bungalows in the country in a rustic setting.

There are only two **campsites** on Gran Canaria, neither of which offers the comfort to be found in their European equivalents: Camping Maspalomas, tel: 767742 and Camping Temisas on the C185 between Agüimes and Santa Lucia, tel: 798149.

Apartments are an option

Visitors should note that hotel tariffs vary considerably according to season.

Beware of sharks

Newly arrived visitors toying with the idea of making Gran Canaria their second home should beware of the representatives of time-sharing organisations – usually young and suntanned. They approach visitors with the idea of introducing them to this apparently inexpensive method of acquiring a holiday home. Too late it may occur to the visitor that the interest payments on the investment alone would have financed a holiday, even without the additional charges for administration, maintenance and repairs. Protests, however, are pointless, as to date there is no right of withdrawal under Spanish law if the purchaser has second thoughts.

Hotel selection

The following are suggestions for some of the most popular spots. They are listed according to the following price categories: $$$ = expensive; $$ = moderate; $ = cheap.

Agaete
$Casa Tecla, Concepción, tel: 898166. This inexpensive alternative to the spa hotel Princesa Guayarmina (*see*

below) will appeal to nature lovers and walkers wishing to explore the Agaete Valley. The hotel lies in the centre of the town and offers just three attractive, clean rooms and one *apartamento*.

Bahía Feliz
$$$Orquidea, Playa de Tarajalillo, tel: 764600. The hotel is like the resort itself: young, sporty and luxurious.

Barranco de Agaete (Los Berrazales)
$$Hotel Princesa Guayarmina, Barrio Los Berrazales, tel: 898009, fax: 898525. The stylish spa hotel at the end of the romantic gorge is no longer an insider tip. Visitors from Las Palmas make the trek, especially at weekends, not least because of the good food. Book in advance.

Las Hoyas (Moya)
$$Earthways, El Cortijo, Las Hoyas, tel: 610654. This country house-cum-bed-and-breakfast establishment is in many respects unique. It is owned by an English couple who organise pottery and weaving courses and expertly guided climbing and mountain-bike tours. There are only a handful of rooms which are often fully booked, so it is essential to make a reservation well in advance.

Las Palmas
$$$Los Bardinos, Eduardo Bonet 5, tel: 266100, fax: 229139. The tower block, over 100 (320ft) high, is almost a city landmark. The 215 rooms are functional rather than attractive. Request a room on one of the upper floors, not just for the view, but because the journey to the rooftop swimming pool is shorter, and the noise of the traffic less disturbing. **$$$Melía**, Gomera 4, tel: 267600, fax: 268411. The largest hotel in town, with more than 300 rooms, is right on the beach. Not necessarily the most elegant address, but certainly the most expensive. Offers the standard to be expected from a five-star establishment. **$$$Reina Isabel**, Alfredo L. Jones 40, tel: 260100, fax: 274558. The 'noble house' boasts the prettiest garden for miles around, a very good restaurant, a first-class location on the Playa de las Canteras and all the amenities of a five-star hotel. **$$$Santa Catalina**, Parque Doramas, tel: 243140, fax: 242764. Celebrities stay here when they come to town. The oldest hotel on Gran Canaria is furnished with antiques. The tranquil Doradas Park compensates for the otherwise slightly inconvenient location. **$$Atlanta**, Alfredo L. Jones 37, tel: 265062. This family hotel near the Playa de las Canteras has good shops in the vicinity and offers reduced rates during the summer. **$$Gran Canaria**, Paseo de las Canteras 38, tel: 275078. Has 90 rooms directly on the beach, all quiet and with bathroom, radio and

The Santa Catalina

telephone. Even pets are allowed. **$Madrid**, Plaza Cairasco 2, tel: 360664. The house itself is old-fashioned, although some people describe it as 'historic'. The 40 rooms are hardly nobly equipped: some don't even have a bathroom. And yet the colonial-style hotel between the historic Vegueta and Triana districts is popular, much-loved and often full.

Dunes of Maspalomas

Maspalomas
$$$Royal Maspalomas Oasis, Playa de Maspalomas, tel: 141448, fax: 141192. The best hotel in the island, with high prices. **$$$IFA Faro Hotel**, Plaza del Faro, tel: 142214, fax: 141940. A four-star hotel close to the beach with two swimming pools and bungalows. **$$Eugenia Victoria**, Avenida de Gran Canaria 26, tel: 762260. Not new, but not too expensive either. Central, but noisy.

Faro Hotel

Playa del Inglés
$$$Posada Mirador, Direccíon Roas, Official Mayor José Rubio 1, tel: 127152. Located in the mountains above Playa del Inglés with a magnificent view. **$$$Apolo**, Avenida de Estados Unidos 28, tel: 760058, fax: 763918. The service of a four-star hotel has its price. Rather noisy location. **$$$Arco Iris**, Milán 11, tel: 762170. Breath-taking view and near the dunes. Expensive. **$$Sahara Playa**, Playa, tel: 760162. Quiet and inexpensive.

Puerto de Mogán
$$Club de Mar, tel: 565066, fax: 565438. Attractively furnished hotel which also rents similar holiday flats throughout the village. **$$Casa Lila**, tel: 565403. On the far side of the bay, run by a German proprietress.

San Agustín
$$$Inter Club Atlantic, Jazmines 2, tel: 760950, fax: 760974. The largest holiday-flat complex is also the most expensive and the best. It is sometimes difficult for indi-vidual travellers to reserve accommodation as develop-ments of this kind are mostly booked en bloc by package-tour operators. **$$$Meliá Tamarindos**, Retama 3, tel: 762600, fax: 762264. Ideal for surfers and gamblers (casino on site, identification required), as well as for high-income tourists. One of the two five-star hotels on the Costa Canaria. **$$Rocas Rojas**, San Agustín, tel: 761621. Almost as elegant, but less expensive.

Santa Brígida
$$$Hotel Golf Bandama, Contrada Bandama, Santa Brígida, tel: 353354, fax: 351290. Very small and im-maculately maintained. The prices in this luxury hotel are correspondingly high (green fees included).

Index